Goodbye, Perfect

HOW TO STOP PLEASING, PROVING, AND PUSHING FOR OTHERS...AND

Live For Yourself

HOMAIRA KABIR

simple truths
▶ Small books. BIG IMPACT.

Copyright © 2023 by Homaira Kabir
Cover and internal design © 2023 by Sourcebooks
Cover design by Jillian Rahn/Sourcebooks
Lettering by Christine Webster
Cover image © amtitus/Getty Images

Sourcebooks, Simple Truths, and the colophon are registered trademarks of Sourcebooks.

This publication is designed to provide accurate and authoritative information in regard
to the subject matter covered. It is sold with the understanding that the publisher is not
engaged in rendering legal, accounting, or other professional service. If legal advice
or other expert assistance is required, the services of a competent professional person
should be sought.—*From a Declaration of Principles Jointly Adopted by a Committee
of the American Bar Association and a Committee of Publishers and Associations*

All brand names and product names used in this book are trademarks,
registered trademarks, or trade names of their respective holders. Sourcebooks
is not associated with any product or vendor in this book.

Published by Simple Truths, an imprint of Sourcebooks
P.O. Box 4410, Naperville, Illinois 60567-4410
(630) 961-3900
sourcebooks.com

Library of Congress Cataloging-in-Publication Data is on file with the publisher.

Printed and bound in the United States of America.
VP 10 9 8 7 6 5 4 3 2 1

To Ammi Abajan

Contents

Introduction

Before We Begin

So you faced a setback or made a mistake. Or someone else had a win or got a piece of great news. And now that voice in your head is having a heyday. It's reminding you that you failed, or that you're way behind. That *you* are a failure. And everyone else is on top of their game.

So you try harder. You set bigger goals. You raise the bar on yourself. You pile even more on to your to-do list, even though you're already burning out.

For a while, things look good. The desire to be in control is motivating. You secretly compare yourself to others and silently pat yourself on the back. The success, praise, approval, or productivity makes you feel ~~good~~ great. You're addicted.

And then something happens. You get negative feedback. Maybe things don't go as planned. Or someone else does better or looks happier. Or maybe the success or praise feels undeserving or not enough. You suddenly feel down. Maybe angry. Maybe ashamed.

You have no choice but to try harder. Because for competent and conscientious women, giving up is not an option.

Welcome to the emotional roller-coaster world of fragile confidence.

I was nearing my fortieth birthday when it struck me that life was passing me by, and I had yet to step fully into it. I'd been feeling this way for a while, but the daily grind of raising four kids while setting up a coaching business had kept me from paying close attention. Who has time, much less the energy, for the more soulful questions when getting through the day is its own ordeal?

Now that the kids were getting older and the business had taken off somewhat, I had time to think about the life I was living and the life I wanted to live.

The life I was living was full of *shoulds* and *have tos*. *I should have more patience. I should've prepared better. I have to start a podcast if I want my business to grow.* I felt I was on a treadmill, where the speed and incline only went one way: up. And all the running in the world didn't get me any closer to the ease and joy I so desperately wanted to experience.

I wanted to be present in life's journey, have time to laugh, notice the bird pecking outside my window, sit with my child, friend, or neighbor without worrying about the work I still had to do. I wanted to live with more grace but also more grit instead of doubting myself and comparing my coaching business with those who were making a bigger impact through their work. I loved what I did, but I kept stumbling over myself trying to get somewhere faster than I could go. And I was tired of the endless running.

When I turned forty, that dissonance suddenly was at the forefront of my mind. What was missing? Why was I stuck in this space of trying harder and harder yet feeling forever behind? What would bring me the joy and meaning I longed to experience, not just in fleeting moments but as a more lasting sense of fulfillment? What would help me occupy a bigger space in my own life?

COMMON PAINS

Around the time I was grappling with these questions, I could see my coaching clients struggling with much of the same. Women's lives are, after all, woven through with the same threads. Our unfair share of challenges have raised our conscience. We long to grow into the best version of ourselves not to stoke the ego, but to leave the world a little better than we found it.

The women I worked with knew something was missing from their lives, but they either didn't quite know what it was or didn't have the courage to pursue it wholeheartedly. There was ambivalence (*I'm not sure if this is a good idea*). There was self-doubt (*I don't think I can really do this*). And there was a whole lot of self-criticism; they'd beat down on themselves for *knowing* what to do and still not doing it or for doing it and falling short of some self-prescribed standard they knew was unreasonable.

One day, a client said to me, "My greatest wish right now is that I make a mistake and shrug it off with *yeah, whatever*. My sister does it all the time, but I just can't. I don't know what's wrong with me." I knew that voice of being "wrong" or "lacking" all too well. Despite having multiple coaching credentials, I still wondered whether I was good enough to be a coach. And these feelings came through not just in the conversations I had with my clients and how far I was willing to challenge toward their goals, but also in how comfortable I was charging appropriately for my services. It's all too common for women to measure our worth through money and put a dismal price on it.

I knew that to help my clients experience the breakthroughs they wanted, I had to embody the courage I was expecting from them. They were competent, qualified, and successful women. No doubt, they faced many, many unfair barriers to their growth, and it was worse for women of color or those who identified with other aspects of intersectionality. But all too often, it was their own expectations of themselves that seemed to cripple them.

There was Priyanka, who was heading global operations at an international fintech company and in charge of decisions that impacted hundreds of people around the world. You would think her position would have given her the courage to take bold action. Instead, she said she constantly felt like a fraud. "I wake up every morning wanting to quit," she said. "I feel I've had a good run, and I'd better walk away before I'm found out."

Another highly successful client, who starred as the main character in a very popular TV show in the nineties, felt debilitated by similar feelings. Even though her career was long over, she continued to have a dream that had haunted her for decades. "I have this recurring nightmare. I'm on the set as [the character she played]. I'm in the midst of a very emotional scene when the director walks in and pulls off my hair wig. 'You're not [the character]' he says. 'The game is over.' That's when I always wake up in a sweat."

Were we, as competent and conscientious women, destined to crawl our way to the top, only to be unhappy if or when we got there? I thought of many of the successful women I'd met and worked with in the developing countries I'd lived in for a large part of my life. They had grown up in cultures where they faced social, institutional, and interpersonal challenges that were far more repressive than the ones most of my clients or I were facing. As little girls, they'd been given a fraction of the education, experiences, and opportunities that most of us had received. As adults, they constantly came up against closed doors and systemic barriers enough to crush the most heartfelt ambition. But their grit was still intact.

I remember Mama Maggie, a Tanzanian tour guide I met when she visited my children's school in Oman, where we were living at the time. I was infatuated by her infectious joy and the presence with which she listened to others. I was also in awe of her spirit; she ran the Dare Women's Foundation, which she started to provide free sanitary pads to girls and women. As a child, she'd lived through the harrowing experience of being beaten by her teacher when her period had leaked because makeshift cloth pads was all they had in their village.

In her foundation, she also taught English to women so they could get better jobs. In the initial days, the men in the village would shout insults at her, attack her home and foundation, and do all they could to stop her. Instead of being fazed by the opposition, Mama Maggie's dedication to her cause grew stronger every day, and she set about understanding the real reason the men were upset. When she found that it was the fear of losing control over their wives, she began educating them on the financial benefits of having dual incomes and how it would actually make them more in control of their lives.

That was when I began becoming obsessed by this thought: *What would it take for us to grow into the biggest version of ourselves without tormenting ourselves along the way? How could we experience more joy, more ease, more grace despite the challenges along the way?* What did Mama Maggie and others like her have that the rest of us didn't? Was it confidence? After all, it was the one quality every client wanted, regardless of why she came to me for coaching. Even the ones who seemed pretty self-assured would talk about their "crisis of confidence" when presented with a new challenge or when someone doubted their performance or intentions. Was confidence really the path to more joy, more success, more meaning, and a bigger impact in the world through our unique strengths and qualities?

I decided to find out.

TWO FORMS OF HIGH CONFIDENCE

I went back to graduate school to study positive psychology (the science of an actualized life) and coaching psychology (the science of helping people create real change in their lives). For my dissertation, I naturally chose to research women's confidence with this question in mind: *Does confidence lead to self-actualization?*

I didn't realize at the time what a conundrum I was stepping into. Confidence is one of the most contested fields of psychological study, with as many definitions as there are scientists studying it. In the scientific literature, there's no unified definition of what it is and how it develops. It's been called *self-esteem, self-worth, self-efficacy, self-care, self-compassion*, and much else by those who study or teach it. Researchers disagree on where it comes from, how we build it, and whether it's even a quality worth pursuing. The failed self-esteem movements of the 1970s brought to light an ugly side of confidence: narcissistic behaviors resulting from excessive coddling and praise because "everyone is a winner."

My mission with the research became twofold:

1. Find a psychological definition of confidence that speaks to the needs, challenges, and aspirations of women in the twenty-first century.

2. Develop an evidence-based framework to build it so we can let go of the tyranny of striving harder and *joyfully* reach for our biggest lives.

Instrumental to my research was the scientific literature developed by the late Michael H. Kernis, whose work in social and personal psychology led him to coin two forms of high self-esteem: *fragile self-esteem* and *optimal self-esteem*.[1] Although they can sometimes look quite similar on the outside, the difference lies in the *implicit* sense we carry about our sense of self-worth.

In fragile confidence, the implicit sense is less than optimal, even though we may not know it. But it's reflected in our behaviors (perfection, endless performing, comparison or competition, seeking praise, approval and permission...), and in our emotions. We experience stress, anxiety and comparison in our pursuits, and shame and depression when we fall behind or do not come out on top, even if our standards may have been quite unreasonable.

Optimal confidence, on the other hand, is underpinned by a deep-seated sense of self-trust in our enough-ness and our ability to impact the world, be it in some small way. It's independent of specific outcomes, achievements, or feedback and is psychologically uplifting because it is "reciprocally related" to authenticity. We feel alive because we're showing up as our best selves in pursuit of what we want and not what someone else wants or expects of us. This is the journey of self-actualization.

It was sadly obvious that fragile confidence is what most of us have. And it was clearly evident that optimal confidence is what we desperately want, not just for our own well-being and fulfillment but also for a troubled world that needs more of us showing up with the drive and passion of intrinsic motivation.

Beyond a definition though, the scientific literature left me hanging. Unfortunately, I found no proven framework that built the components of optimal confidence. The reason was understandable; confidence is difficult to measure given its implicit nature. And measurement is a key element of scientific design.

It was up to me to create the framework.

FINDING THE WAY

Positive psychology changes you in ways you never imagine, because unlike other disciplines, it forces you to **live what you learn**. In the years that followed my studies, I came face-to-face with more fears than I knew I had. And I had to find ways to *move through them*, because moving around them simply expands their reach.

There was one fear in particular that was keeping me from the framework I knew I needed to create. It was the fear of sounding less rational, less analytical, and thus, to my mind, less educated to my peers and clients. For the longest time, I'd hidden my softer, more emotional, more soulful side under a mask of *intellectualization* for fear I would sound a little "woo-woo." We do, after all, live in a world where knowledge is the domain of the head and where we can judge others and ourselves as weak for engaging the heart.

I remember the time I was invited to give a TEDx talk on human goodness. Writing the talk had been a breeze. But I struggled with the delivery, because it's impossible for me to talk about human goodness without welling up with tears. My children—always my first audience—sat through rounds and rounds of practice with me choking on my words. "Mom, you can't cry," they implored. They knew I'd done so in the past. And those memories still haunted them.

It was during a parenting course at their school, when I was called up on stage to talk about Randy Pausch's touching last lecture. Randy Pausch was a professor of computer science and design at Carnegie Mellon University, who learned, at age forty-five, that he had pancreatic cancer and only a few months to live. His last lecture was his parting words to his family, friends, and students on how to live a good life.

I'd barely begun talking when I felt the force of emotions well up inside me. I panicked and desperately tried to recall practical takeaways from the talk so I could disengage my heart.

It didn't work. The more I suppressed my emotions, the stronger they came on. Before I knew it, I was seconds away from bursting into tears. In a last-ditch effort at face saving, I blurted out, "I miss Randy!" And with that, I collapsed into sobs.

There was pin-drop silence for a while as the shocked parent community looked on. They likely wondered whether I'd known Randy Pausch in any capacity other than the one video we'd watched together. I hadn't, but I pray to God they believed I had. Luckily, the principal rushed to my rescue and carried me to my seat. I'll forever be grateful to her for that.

Having learned from that fateful delivery, I pared out every emotional phrase from my TEDx talk. Even so, I came this close to a Randy Pausch replay on the actual day. My voice shook, my throat buckled, and more than once, I paused at the most inopportune moment to gather myself. My only solace is that I was able to walk off the stage on my own two feet.

Friends who had graciously come to cheer me on came up to me during the break with a smile that said *You want to talk?* One of them consoled me with "At least it's over." Another reminded me: "It was your first time." I think what he failed to understand was that it was my *every* time.

~~~~~

My parents visited from abroad a few weeks later. One morning after breakfast, my father brought out a carefully packaged bundle of sheets of paper. They were yellow with age and seemed to contain what looked like calligraphy. "It's your great-grandfather's journal," my father said. I made tea, and we went out in the backyard to read it together.

As my father read it aloud, I felt myself transported to a life I'd never known nor will ever experience. But then came a paragraph that spoke to that something deep inside that longed for a more beautiful world. It's how author Susan Cain explains unexplainable and spontaneous tears in her latest book *Bittersweet*. The paragraph began, "Father would weep uncontrollably as he read Rumi at sundown."[2] And it went on to describe the impact the

Sufi poet's words had on my great-great-grandfather. My father's voice shook. My throat hurt. And one thing was clear: I come from a long line of weepers who feel the pain of our common human suffering and who are moved to tears by the potential in human goodness.

I wish I'd known all this before the talk. I may have had an easier time with the delivery. I may have allowed myself a few tears instead of vying for the perfect talks I'd been ogling for months. I may even have been able to look myself in the eyes, smile at my quirky emotions, and say with a nod of approval, *Hey, I like you.*

SCIENCE WITH A SOUL

The fear of exposing a hidden part of me returned when I was building the framework. Even though the research on confidence being an implicit construct was clear, I doubted myself. Even though the science was equivocal that the implicit world is inaccessible to conscious thought and reasoning, my ambivalence was loud. *Will my road map appeal to the corporate and professional women who would be the main beneficiaries? Will my clients find it too soft and unrelatable to the daily challenges of work and life? Will my field value it as an important contribution or reject me as a renegade?* My inner critic was having a blast.

Luckily, this time around, I had tools to manage it. It was, after all, what the framework was all about: to find the courage *within* to **brave on** toward intrinsically driven goals despite the fears, self-doubt, setbacks, and criticism along the way. I was being called to live it. That's what callings do—they bring us face-to-face with the darkness and the shadows we need to let go of. And in doing so, they help us claim our place to stand, our voice to raise, our light to shine in the world.

And thus the framework came into being.

Hundreds of women have been through it, both in my coaching work and in the randomized controlled trials I ran as part of my postgraduate research. The transformations have been magical: careers advanced, businesses launched, books written, communities started, relationships repaired, promotions asked for and accepted, and promotions declined in favor of a better opportunity or a life that feels truer and more fulfilling.

I've been incredibly heartened by these transformational changes. Because if there's one thing that's clear, it's that the extent of growth in any area of our lives—professional, relational, or communal—depends on our personal growth. The higher our aspirations or the greater our challenges, the more the drive to secure our safety. It's human, built into us through millennia of biological evolution.

The only way we rise to our greatest potential, despite the obstacles on the way, is by becoming aware of the fears, resentments, beliefs, and gifts—yes, gifts—that are embedded in our bones. Because there's a basic tenet in psychology: our ability to rise to our challenges depends on the resources we have to do so.

Finding, owning, and building our inner resources is so important for women, because we lose touch with them as we go through life. There's no end of messaging on who we should be, guideposts on how to belong, criticism for embracing who we are, and rewards for rejecting parts of ourselves others don't like. We learn that to be worthy of love and acceptance, we need to be a certain way.

Ultimately, the messages become conflicting, the rewards stop coming, and we're brought face-to-face with ourselves. Although painful and disorienting, it's a moment ripe with possibility. As research scholar Dr. Lisa Miller writes in her book *The Awakened Brain*, moments of transition are a call to connect within.[3] When we do, we move closer to flourishing. And when we don't have a way of doing so, we languish.

This is especially true for working women as they rise in seniority. And yet, there's no leadership development program to meet them at the crossroads. They're left to figure out the way forward on their own, and boy is that hard, given the relentless messaging and endless to-do lists. But the reality is that our inner world is essential for our outer leadership, especially in a world defined by uncertainty, complexity, and change. The better we know ourselves, more courageous we are in our pursuits, because we have the strength of our truth to hold us steady through the challenges and complexities of life.

That is optimal confidence.

⌐⌐⌐⌐

I want to briefly describe the journey you're about to take.

Part 1 will help you build an understanding of why your confidence may be fragile, how that fragility shows up in your life, and the gaps you need to address to build a lasting sense of confidence. This is the essential step that's often missing when we simply tell people what to do. Our behaviors, however unhelpful, create some sense of reward in our brains. Unless we understand the false promise of a reward that underpins these behaviors and the reality of how *un*rewarding they really are for the lives we want to live, we cannot let go of them.

Parts 2 and 3 are about building the two essential and sequential components of confidence. Each part comprises two chapters that address the component from the from the inside out and the outside in respectively. With each of the four chapters, you'll also be building an inner presence that will help you build the component even when it is hard, because the map is not territory. You will need this presence beside you as you make your way through the terrain. I absolutely love teaching this material because I see women transforming before my very eyes.

Each component builds upon the previous one, so go through them in order. Later, you can come back to them as you please, depending on what you're facing in your life, because confidence is not an item on a to-do list, complete once you've ticked it off. We live in a world that will always challenge the limits of our patience and courage while reminding us of ways we fall short. To experience this precious life fully, and grow into the best version of ourselves, getting back up, brushing ourselves off, and continuing the journey is the work of a lifetime.

Part 4 is about the change in perspective that emerges as the roots of confidence take hold. It's like the seedlings you've nurtured have sprouted, and the bud that is you is opening up to experience more of the world in all its paradoxes. The joys along with the jolts. The *little* joys the world offers us right here, right now, that we often overlook. Because it's the little things that will help us face the suffering and pain within us and around us that are calling us to *turn to* and not against. To move forward and not away. To break open and not apart.

GROWING UP

We all hear the wake-up call at some point in our lives. It can come from a sudden widening of our perspective—of catching a glimpse of our brilliance we didn't know existed, of that precious wild animal inside that takes us by surprise. Or from the breathtaking sight of the rising sun or an early morning walk in the wilderness that reminds us there's more to life than our dogged and draining pursuits.

It can also come from the *longing* for a wider perspective. From despair, from feeling besieged and burned out. From the loss of a loved one or of the life we knew. From repeated setbacks and failures, and sometimes a single one. It can even come from success and realizing that it brought none of the happiness we were looking for.

A lot of us experienced this during the COVID-19 pandemic. In the initial days, there was a sense of suddenly waking up, realizing that our ways were not working, and committing to a life lived from the inside out. But for many, it didn't last that long, certainly not long enough to consistently put it into practice. As the world picked up speed again, we began running with it. Running faster and faster so we don't fall behind. Just as we'd always done.

We had woken up, perhaps because the world had given us a breather to do so. But as author Ken Wilber, developer of integral thinking, cautions, it is not enough to wake up; it is also necessary to grow up.[4] This book offers you a path to do so. I've shared everything I've learned about the science of flourishing (and what gets in women's way), including evidence-based tools to live with joy, integrity, and courage. There are plenty of personal and professional stories for you to relate with, including those that will lift you up even in your moments of darkness—the kind of stories I wish the younger me had known when she struggled alone. And I've woven it all together with both my heart and my hope that the book impacts your life for the better.

As an aside, many kind and conscientious men, who have been on my mailing list for years and benefited from the work I do, have asked me whether the book is for them too. Here's what I say to them: if something is keeping you from living the life you want to live, this book is for you. If you want to stop hurting yourself so much in the pursuit of what others value or society rewards, this book is for you. If you see personal growth as the pathway to professional growth and relational fulfillment, this book is for you.

There's a transformation in human consciousness taking place in our world, where there's a heightened hunger for soulful self-actualization across genders. I want you to know that the journey to your best self is not only possible, it is imperative that you take it. Because hearing the call and going back to sleep may appease you for a while. Alas, the world offers many ways to keep us busy and distracted.

But there will come a day when you'll ask yourself what you did with your one wild and precious life. My wish for you, dear reader, is that you'll be able to look yourself in the eye and say: *I lived.*

Thank you for the trust you've placed in me.

Part I

Understanding Fragile Confidence

Chapter 1

The Gap of Fragile Confidence

I was eight when I got my first gold star. My third-grade teacher had held my notebook up in front of the class as an example of perfect handwriting. I felt the rush of pride, of feeling seen and validated, loved almost. But on the heels of it, I also felt the gaze of fifty classmates, and my cheeks turned hot with embarrassment. *What if I can never do it again? They'll think I'm such a fraud. Should I tell them it was a fluke?* The limelight blinded me.

More importantly, I worried about what they were thinking. *Were they jealous? Would they hate me for it? What if they didn't let me play with them at recess or share their secrets with me anymore?* I desperately wished my teacher had silently slipped the star inside my desk rather than make a public display of it.

Luckily, no one really cared. One of my friends was also a neighbor, and her only ask was that I not tell her parents. I later learned they compared her to me all the time, and she'd had enough of it. With my classmates' feelings and judgment out of the way, I was free to collect as many gold stars as I could. Correction: I *had* to collect as many stars as I could, because the bar had been raised for me. And it only kept going higher.

From that day on, I'd spend hours writing, erasing, and rewriting each letter so my homework looked like a work of art. Sometimes the pages would tear with all the erasing and tears of frustration, and I'd have to begin all over again. Friends down the street would come to get me in the evenings so we could go out and play. Most times, they'd leave without me because I was still toiling over my homework. Over time, they stopped coming.

I'd found a new friend: perfection. She had a couple of loyal buddies: praise and approval. We became close, hanging out together all the time. When I felt lonely or missed my old friends, they always came to the rescue. *Let's try harder* was a game they loved to play. I became very good at it. So good that I soon forgot about the joy and connection I traded in for it.

It's a story many of us are familiar with. I've been coaching women for over ten years now, and if there's one thread that weaves through almost every story, it's perfection, sometimes visible and debilitating and sometimes expressed as a desire to find more joy and meaning in our lives. Somewhere on the journey to growing up, we parked our hearts, hoping to return to them once we'd sorted everything else out.

The things kept on coming. Investing in a home. Putting the kids through college. Saving for retirement. By the time they stopped (if they stopped), we'd lost sight of the parking lot.

Shortly after my research on confidence as the wellspring of flourishing, I began offering coaching circles for women. I always began with this question: **What will having more confidence mean to you?** The answers were varied:

I'll write that book I've always wanted to write.

I'll leave my job and travel for a year to find myself.

I'll be able to set boundaries with people and say no when I need to.

I'll leave my partner and look for a relationship that makes me happy.

I'll take time to figure out what I really want because I have no clue.

I'll stop asking for permission to do the little things I love.

I'll start my own cupcake shop and not worry about wasting my degree in law.

I'll stop obsessing over whether my son will care about me once he leaves home.

Embedded in each of them was the longing for freedom, to break away from what others would think and *choose* how they wanted to live their lives.

THE PERENNIAL PURSUIT

There was a follow-up question I would ask in my coaching circles: **How have you tried to build your confidence?** I was surprised by how much this question would throw the women off. Some would say they'd never really tried; they didn't know how to. "Isn't it like you kind of have it or you don't?" they would ask. Others would say they'd done everything in their power—read books, done courses and workshops—and nothing had helped. "I think it's me. I just don't have what it takes." That thought was certainly not going to help.

Most of them, though, would talk about how they were doing more and trying harder, even though they kind of knew it wasn't helping. Maddie had been an ophthalmologist for the past twenty years. Despite oodles of experience, she didn't feel confident to take on a bigger role at the clinic, and had been piling up additional certifications, thinking that would help. When it didn't, she wondered whether it was the profession and began training as a coach on the side. At the session, she shared she was more confused than ever and had recently signed up with a burnout coach.

Juhi, who was in her fifties and ran a profitable merchandise business, felt that an intimate relationship would give her the confidence she lacked. She signed up on various dating platforms, but given the prejudice against older women, didn't get the interest she was hoping for. The two times someone did reach out to her, she was so desperate to make it work that she likely scared them away. The only "suitor" who hung on long enough turned out to be a scam artist who would target rich older women, win their trust, and then ask for money. "A part of me figured out what was going on. But I kept going along with it because it felt good to have him in my life. I didn't want him to leave."

Then there was Clare, who knew that her need to be liked was slowing down her work. She would toil over emails to her team that she could've written in minutes if she didn't parse every sentence and worry how it would make them feel. This would create a backlog of the work she actually enjoyed as a creative director, and staying back to finish it would lead to needless bickering with her girlfriend at home.

When she'd tried to be efficient with her emails, she not only found it gut-wrenchingly hard, but she also wasted time obsessing about whether she had offended someone. Sometimes she'd apologize needlessly and then feel worse about herself for not being poised and leaderlike. She had carved an identity that she couldn't break out of and felt caught in a rut; even doing the "right thing," with all the courage it took, brought her no respite. Her only choice was to become a "better" version of the existing Clare, a Clare 2.0. Not a transformed Clare. Not one who could relate *differently* with her world.

Maddie, Juhi, and Clare are among the millions of women who are burning themselves out to prove themselves in some way, and sometimes to their own selves. Why the need to do so?

A BOTTOMLESS PIT

The scientific literature developed by the late Michael H. Kernis informed much of my research on confidence. His work on self-esteem at the Department of Psychology and Institute for Behavioral Research at the University of Georgia led him to uncover two types of *high* self-esteem: fragile self-esteem and optimal self-esteem. We'll call them *fragile confidence* and *optimal confidence* (or simply *confidence*) respectively in this book.

Fragile confidence is different from *low* confidence, where our conscious thoughts and beliefs about ourselves tend to be negative. Instead, it's *positive* thoughts and self-evaluations that lack a deep-seated sense of trust in the goodness in our hearts and the gifts our lives embody. Sometimes, fragile confidence can even look like excessive self-assurance.

Optimal confidence, on the other hand, is a healthy alignment of what we think and how we feel about ourselves. We're far less impacted by negative feedback, because it's mitigated by that intuitive trust we have in our sense of self-worth.

This trust doesn't live in our heads; it's a "felt sense" that lives in the more inaccessible parts of our brains, also called the *implicit* or *subconscious world*. As such, it's visceral, irrational, logically indefensible, and resistant to feedback that doesn't align with it. When we trust that regardless of success, failure, and praise or criticism, we are worthy of being loved and valued for who we are, we can go after our heartfelt desires without stressing so much about what others would think or say.

When we receive positive feedback (success, praise, moments of connection, etc.) we're not driven to shout our achievements from the rooftops because it's not news to our subconscious brains. We can evaluate ourselves positively (*I'm a good person, I did the right thing, I'm strong at presentations*), and these positive self-evaluations naturally sink into our implicit memory because they're aligned with our internal stories about ourselves. And when we don't get positive feedback—we all get our fair share of failures and criticism, especially when pursuing any worthwhile endeavor—we don't spiral down into shame and blame, because we have the buffers of our implicit beliefs to break the fall.

Say your mom casually says something negative about your parenting. Nothing huge, maybe a passing remark that your little one's eczema is because you didn't drink enough milk during your pregnancy (only moms can make that connection!). Or that if you spent more time with your teenager, she wouldn't sulk as much as she does (teenagers sulk, full stop). Of course, you get triggered. Of course, you want to tell your mom to keep her opinions to herself. Maybe you also start questioning your parenting or feeling guilty about the eczema or the sulking. None of this is wrong. In fact, it would be weird if you didn't feel anything. Our emotions show that we care.

But trusting your goodness and capabilities provides a safe landing for negative feedback, because it doesn't feed it with your own. You can take other people's comments or life's setbacks in stride, place them in the larger picture, learn from them if you need to, and let go of them if you don't. As Jonathan Brown at the University of Washington explained, self-trust allows you to fail without feeling bad about yourself.

THE PERPETUAL YO-YO

Without empowering implicit beliefs, we become dependent on external feedback to feel good *about ourselves*. The approval-seeking, the proving, and the addiction to praise, pleasing, perfection, power, productivity, or a combination of them all are about concealing an inner inadequacy or shame that we may or may not be aware of. **They're about a felt sense that we're not worthy of love and acceptance unless we're doing something that makes us so.**

When we receive positive feedback for our efforts, our

self-evaluations and emotions in the moment are positive, sometimes excessively so, because they aren't aligned with what we intuitively believe about ourselves. Perhaps we've surprised ourselves, and we want the whole world to know about it! This is the high of fragile confidence, buoyed by praise, approval, and success.

Even so, none of these accolades, nor our resulting self-evaluations, impact the implicit world, because it's immune to what doesn't match its unspoken story. The deep-seated sense of unworthiness (shame or inadequacy) stays intact. And the need for positive feedback continues to grow. If the positive feedback is indeed incessant, the gap between positive self-evaluations and negative implicit beliefs widens, and fragile confidence bears an uncanny resemblance with narcissistic behaviors.

Most women don't need to fear this extreme outcome, because few people walk around with a tiara to place on our heads. Not just in workplaces but also in our personal lives. And asking for one, even when we've proven ourselves to be deserving of it, doesn't go down well either. Most of us can relate to the experience of having been called needy, demanding, or brash simply for speaking up for ourselves. Time and again, we're reminded, in subtle and not-so-subtle ways, to shoulder the responsibility for other people's setbacks or to give away credit for our achievements so our playing big doesn't ruffle any feathers. We're told to curb our ambitions and be grateful for what we have, which works because of a feminine sensibility to the anguish and suffering in the world. The fear of becoming too big for our britches is hardly something that should keep us up at night.

Our experience of fragile confidence is more like being on an emotional roller-coaster of high and low confidence. Negative feedback touches upon a perceived and painful truth that isn't far from conscious awareness because of constant reminders of how we fail to measure up in some, usually undefined, way. Instead of feeling bad or unhappy, we feel ashamed or depressed, because we're feeding the external judgment with our own. Some of us beat down on ourselves or engage in pleasing and appeasing behaviors, the classic low confidence response. Others blame, dismiss, justify, or seek sympathy, common reactions in fragile confidence. For women in particular, shame and blame are two sides of the same coin and often happen together.

A WOMAN'S EXPERIENCE OF FRAGILE CONFIDENCE

⊖ WHAT WE THINK/BELIEVE ⊕

LOW CONFIDENCE ⟵ YO-YO ⟶ FRAGILE CONFIDENCE

⊖ WHAT WE FEEL ⊖

Positive feedback on the other hand, despite the initial high, triggers one of two common patterns. The classic fragile confidence reaction is to try and mine the positive feedback in subtle ways, like overplaying the challenges we faced or being stingy with the credit we give to our teams or to those who helped us succeed. When the praise doesn't match the need for it, we can start feeling unseen and unappreciated, victimized even, which leads to anger or feelings of resentment.

The low confidence response is the dread of being found out to be a fraud, or what we commonly call impostor syndrome. *How will I do this again? It was pure luck. How do I make sure they don't find out?* The research shows that impostor syndrome is highly correlated with low confidence because positive feedback doesn't match our *conscious* negative beliefs. Research also shows that it is highly correlated with a yo-yoing sense of confidence, which is how fragile confidence shows up for most women.[5]

It's why most of us stay up at night perfecting a presentation that's ~~good enough~~ already great. Or why we refuse to apply for a job or negotiate a raise until we've amassed more qualifications and more proof than is needed or necessary. We cannot take risks unless we have guaranteed our success, because failure touches upon a painful perceived truth. And the sad reality is that untested beliefs stay intact.

AN UNSPOKEN RESISTANCE

The implicit world is extremely powerful in driving our behaviors because it is the first point of contact with the external world. What happens thereon is a series of automatic events that are purely orchestrated for our survival.

Feedback that we receive from the external world (success, failure, praise, criticism, connection, rejection, etc.), lands on the first of two components of the implicit world: visceral and cognitive. The visceral is the many unprocessed memories that are housed in the body, either because they're too painful to process or because they happened before a child develops a cognitive system capable of putting them into words. From there, the information is channeled through the cognitive component, also called "core beliefs." Most of our core beliefs are formed in the very early years of life, and accessing them is not easy. In fact, trying too hard can cause more harm than good, because the brain is quite good at putting two and two together to create a faulty story.

Core beliefs are rigid and childlike in nature because they form before we develop a more robust, conscious cognitive system capable of making sense of our experiences or seeing the world in shades of gray. They do not hold space for exceptions, nor are they open to the nuances in a situation.

The implicit world has one key job: to use past experiences to predict what's about to happen next and generate an emotion that motivates us to act. None of us has any say or control over its workings; its processes are automatic, urgent, and faster than ever, honed over millennia to ensure our survival. When it senses threat, the emotion it activates is very powerful; there's no time to think when we need to run for our lives.

If you struggle with impostor syndrome, your emotions will be accompanied by your thoughts because they're explicit. If you can manage your emotions, you can work with these thoughts and reason with yourself. You can remind yourself of why you're the right person for the job you want or why having a certain conversation is important for your relationship. It'll still take courage to do so, but at least you have the awareness to begin.

But when beliefs are purely implicit and hidden from conscious awareness, we react almost instantly to our emotions. By the time the relatively slower rational brain catches up, thoughts take on the role of justifying what we did or have decided to do. This is something the human brain does particularly well. In fact, Scottish philosopher David Hume described reason as the "slave of the passions,"[6] passion being the visceral reactions driven by our impulses, beliefs, and emotions.

We can create entire stories in our heads about people and their motives or about life and its injustices to convince ourselves that we're acting rationally or intentionally. And without an understanding of what really drove us to react, our stories feel like the truth and become self-fulfilling prophesies. No wonder some psychologists describe core beliefs as the stories that accompany us from "cradle to grave."

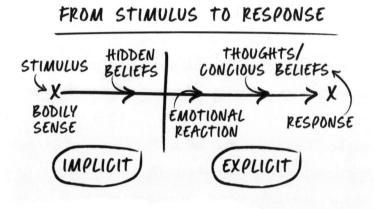

FROM STIMULUS TO RESPONSE

STIMULUS · HIDDEN BELIEFS · THOUGHTS/ CONCIOUS BELIEFS

BODILY SENSE · EMOTIONAL REACTION · RESPONSE

IMPLICIT · EXPLICIT

I'm reminded of Chloe who was a very hardworking and conscientious senior associate at a law firm. She came to me because she felt stuck in her job; she wanted to make partner, but was convinced her boss wasn't going to help her advance. "Three people who joined around the same time as me have already been made partner. I'm more qualified, I've handled more cases where the stakes were high, and she still didn't push my case forward twice when it was time. I'm sure she sees me as a threat."

When we began digging deeper, it turned out that Chloe had never really discussed her professional aspirations with her boss. She had put her head down and worked like a horse, making sure everything was done to perfection. A couple of times in the early days, her boss had even said to her jokingly, "I've become so dependent on you, I'll never want to let you go."

When the promotion didn't happen the first time around, Chloe immediately made up a story that her boss didn't like her. She picked up on every sign that matched her story, and boy is it easy to do that! As neuropsychologist Dr. Rick Hanson writes in his book *Hardwiring Happiness*, the brain is Velcro for what aligns with its stories and Teflon for what doesn't.[7] Chloe's partial attention hurt her relationship with her boss, who, in turn, became disinterested in Chloe's professional growth.

When I asked Chloe whether she had considered bringing up her frustrations or aspirations with her boss, she replied, "I don't know what there is to bring up. My work speaks for itself. No one enters a law firm without the goal of becoming partner—I don't see why I should be asking for it." The more I tried to explain the importance of conveying her strengths and goals, the more resistant she became. "I don't think you understand," she said. "It doesn't work like that." She was stuck in a story from the past, and unable to even see it at play.

When implicit beliefs don't make themselves heard, we keep digging the hole deeper for ourselves because we refuse to take responsibility for our part. Of the two evils, I would rather hear my voice of self-doubt than walk the world as though it owed me something. But luckily we don't have to choose between two evils; we can each walk the world knowing we belong. We can each trust in the deepest recesses of our being that we are worthy of our place in the circle of life. That is the home of optimal confidence.

THE DOWNWARD SPIRAL

When women enter the workplace, they're armed with a formula that's worked for them most of their lives:

$$COMPETENCE + LIKABILITY = CONFIDENCE$$

In the initial stages of their careers, the formula typically continues to apply. Young women are hopeful, they're proactive, they're achievement oriented, and for the most part, they're eager to please. Even those who aren't as relational are rewarded for their performance and for the overt confidence they exude.

They're also at an earlier stage in life, when there's time for friendships, looking after their health and happiness, and pursuing interests outside work. I see it in my oldest daughter and her network of friends and colleagues, who are just a few years out of college. They go to spin class together, they do weekend cookouts, and during the pandemic, three of them formed a "pod" and began offering virtual dance classes.

As most of us who are older know too well, this honeymoon

phase of life doesn't last forever. Sooner or later, life becomes complicated. Families expand and children arrive on the scene. At work, there are more people to lead, higher expectations to meet. This is the second stage of our careers that Dr. Diana Bilimoria at the Weatherhead School of Management, Case Western Reserve University, calls "pragmatic endurance."[8] There's a lot coming at us from all angles, and the endurance requires a lowering of standards and a certain flexibility that's missing when we measure our worth through our performance or the praise we get for it. The well-defined formula that presented a clean path to success begins to flip on its head when we an influx of challenges as we advance in our lives and careers.

Organizational Challenges

Most organizations are meritocracies only up to middle management; the strength of networks determines the path beyond. Between work and raising a family, women generally haven't had the time to develop these networks. They may also feel uncomfortable leveraging their networks, because they've experienced, personally or otherwise, the backlash against ambitious women.

This is also the time when women begin to face ageism, discrimination based on age, which happens sooner than it does for men and hits them harder because it's impacted by "lookism"— discrimination based on societal standards of beauty. Those who do make it to the top can feel like an outsider in the "old boys' club." They're left out of decisions made at the bar or on the golf course because they're likely rushing home to put food on the table. And they aren't part of the conversations that happen beside the water cooler or before the start of a meeting because interests and responsibilities often vary by gender, and there's little common ground beyond small talk.

Jen was a member of the Goodbye Perfect Program, the group coaching program I offer to help women find greater joy and purpose in their lives. At her first session, she shared her reason for joining: "My challenge is not having a sounding board or neutral perspective for work challenges. All my peers are men, and there's only one I would ever talk to about work challenges. I've sometimes shared with a couple of women who report to me when I'm desperate...but I usually regret it, because they need to see me confident."

Structural Challenges

The second stage of a woman's career also coincides with a stage in her life that has often been described as the "burden of motherhood and management." Remember the old saying "little kids, little problems, big kids, big problems"? For working mothers, the problems keep on coming given how adolescence has stretched out at both ends, starting way earlier than it used to and extending all the way into the early twenties. For both mothers and nonmothers, there's also almost always the responsibility of aging parents and/ or in-laws. This can involve long commutes, regular hospital visits, or even time away from work. It also means far less time for the supportive relationships (friends, sisters, neighbors, etc.) that helped them unload their stresses or unpack our emotions.

Our societal structures aren't set up to help women in the role of caregiver. Most of us are hanging on by a thread, something that became starkly evident during the pandemic. Many women were forced to leave jobs after struggling to wear twenty different hats all at once. One of my clients shared how she wore a different set of earbuds in each ear so she could follow two Zoom sessions at the same time—a work meeting and her daughter's online science class.

Interpersonal Challenges

Rare would be the woman who hasn't experienced men speaking over her at meetings, forgetting to acknowledge her voice or contribution, or worse, blatantly taking credit for her ideas. In her 2008 essay "Men Explain Things to Me," writer, historian, and activist Rebecca Solnit describes a conversation with a man who'd just discovered that her latest book was about British photographer Eadweard Muybridge. In her characteristic humor, she writes about how he insisted she read a "very important" Muybridge book. Turns out, it was her book! And he hadn't even read it.

These are not mild irritations. They are the daily paper cuts that "crush young women into silence," says Solnit. "It trains us in self-doubt and self-limitation just as it exercises men's unsupported overconfidence."[9]

A women's career is filled with such paper cuts that are mostly based on cultural biases that are embedded in the social fabric. For example, the classic "John vs. Jennifer" study at Yale showed that women are seen as workers and not leaders, even by other women. And working mothers are seen as less committed and less competent, even though no such thing happens when a man becomes a father. In fact, he rises in stature![10]

These interpersonal challenges take on a whole other dimension as women advance in their careers. The assertiveness that was once rewarded is now seen as "bossy" or "abrasive." And collaboration and compassion become hurdles to advancement because they are seen as "weak". This is the famous "double bind" of competence and likability—damned if you do, and damned if you don't.

Intrapersonal Challenges

This stage is also when women begin to see their careers as an extension of the self. They want to explore the unlived parts of their lives and are caught in a tug between their creative, spiritual, or community pursuits and their professional ones. They're also in midlife, and without adequate support for the physical and mental challenges of menopause (because they don't exist), they can feel exhausted and alone. And yet with everything on their plates, their health and well-being slide to the back burner, adding to their feelings of frustration.

Most of the women who come to me are desperate to find themselves again. They're going through a huge transition—physically, emotionally, cognitively, and spiritually—that holds the potential for monumental personal growth. But without the right resources, they're shutting down at the most basic level. In her book *Silenced and Sidelined*, Dr. Carrie Arnold describes weight gain, sinus and sleep problems, recurring bouts of the cold and flu, and irritating digestive issues as common ailments that plague women when they shut off important aspects of their lives.[11]

LOSING CONFIDENCE

These are the common challenges that almost every woman goes through as she advances in her life and career. And then there may be individual ones such as a child with special needs, a divorce or unhealthy intimate relationship, job loss or financial hardships, an accident or physical disability. Some are able to deal with their challenges by turning inward, reflecting on how they want to live their lives, and then expanding their inner and outer resources to live in alignment with them.

Unfortunately, those with fragile confidence don't have the privilege to do so because *they depend on positive feedback to feel good about themselves.* They know they need to be strategic and focus on the bigger picture. They know that it's impossible to do substantive work of any kind without being open to criticism and failure. They know that their expanding roles require flexibility, and they need to lower their expectations of themselves.

But the moment of truth is rife with intense emotions. Without the underpinning layer of implicit self-worth, it's terribly difficult to let go of what feels safe, even when they *know* it's getting in their way. Initially, they try harder, doing more of what promised them success in the past. But it's no longer that easy. Success at work may mean less time for their health, passions, or with the family. So many successful women blame themselves for their children's mistakes or the way their intimate relationships turned out. Alternately, fulfillment in relationships may come with regrets about their unmet professional potential. As one client said, "I spend most of my time searching old friends and colleagues on LinkedIn and feeling bad about not prioritizing my career."

As positive feedback (from others or our own self-talk) becomes fewer and farther between, implicit beliefs begin to voice themselves or get louder. Self-doubt and self-criticism become more common. Many women start losing the sense of agency they once had, or playing small, even though they may be quick to justify their decisions. This further limits their growth and adds to their pain. All the while, they can sense that something is missing from their lives and they don't have forever to figure out what it is. Hopelessness, shame, and depression begin to set in.

Almost every client I see is at some stage of this long, drawn-out downward spiral. In some form or other, she says, "I've lost the confidence I once had in myself."

Little does she know she never had it.

GRASPING FOR CONTROL

I was almost fourteen when I developed a horrific eating disorder that nearly took my life. My dad had been posted to Senegal, a French-speaking country at the western tip of Africa. He was a diplomat, which meant that our family had moved regularly ever since I was born. I don't remember most of those postings. But the five years spent in Sri Lanka right before Senegal continue to be the best memories of my life.

Moving to Senegal meant saying goodbye to the closest relationships I had. These weren't friends my age—me and my two brothers were mostly homeschooled in Sri Lanka, and most of my time was spent with adults. Overtime, three of them became very special to me.

One was my math teacher, Aunty Coomarasamy, a strong head with a tender heart. When my younger brother (who was definitely gifted at math) and I studied together with her, she didn't go gaga over his math smarts like other teachers had done, because she knew it would neither do him much good, nor help me feel good about my mathematical abilities. Through her gentle nature, she not only helped me gain the confidence in math that I had lost a long time ago, she also became my "bestie" with whom I shared all kinds of girlish dreams.

The second was Aunty Lathifa, my art teacher. For five solid years, I spent almost every afternoon painting in her garage where she held her art classes. Aunty Lathifa had a heart so young that her childlike wonder beamed through her facial expressions. She was the kind of person I needed to restore joy into my life, given the perfectionist I was, with an ever-present inner critic. Once, I spent days at home copying four Picasso masterpieces to a T. They were meant as a surprise for her; I assumed she'd be ecstatic. Instead, she shook her head and said, "Picasso spent his entire life trying to paint like a child. You're a child. I love *your* art."

And then there was Dadima, my precious paternal grandmother who'd lived with us all my life. She was my anchor, my soul mate, and my bedroom partner who would listen to my stories well into the night without an ounce of judgment. To Dadima, there was nothing I could say or do that was wrong. I was perfection itself, simply by token of being her girl.

My mom tells me that when I was born, I was a pretty ugly baby, with slits for eyes and unusually hairy for a newborn. When Dadima came to see me at the hospital (I was in the nursery), my mom described me in much the same way. Dadima retorted right back: "I don't care, she's my daughter." Dadima didn't have any girls of her own.

When my father's Senegal posting was announced, she decided to return to our native Pakistan to live with my uncles. Africa felt too far for her at her age. "I don't want to be buried in a foreign land where no one will be able to visit my grave once you leave," she said. I missed her terribly.

Saying goodbye to the three people who held special places in my heart was doubly hard because I felt I was letting go of them forever. It was another time, remember; travel was rare, mail took forever to reach its destination, and international phone calls were both expensive and cumbersome. It wasn't au revoir. It was adieu.

If it weren't bad enough to lose my resources, my challenges were also about to multiply. I was bumped up two grades in Senegal, because that was the only space available at the school we attended. Two years can feel like a huge gap for friendships when you're thirteen, especially a very innocent thirteen. Besides, it was the middle of the school year, which meant that friend groups were far less porous by this time. I was going through the tough transition into puberty with very little emotional or social support.

These challenges paled in comparison to the real chasm I faced: I had to take the French Baccalaureate exam (equivalent to high school) in less than two years. And I didn't yet speak a word of French!

I felt like a nonswimmer who'd been tossed into the deep end without a lifeline. Being at the bottom of the class upset me *deeply*, because I'd always excelled in my studies. I worked my hardest, trudging through French verbs and pronunciations. But the going was tough and progress painfully slow. I felt stuck and stupid. Through the emotional journey of many losses, sprinkled with a few wins that I refused to celebrate, I began to feel hopeless about my academic success.

I also felt unseen. Teachers had only so much time and patience for someone who was so far behind. And friendships were almost impossible until I'd learned at least some French. In hindsight, I could've made it easier for myself by being willing to speak with my budding language skills. But that was a permission I refused to give myself. The horror of making a mistake, of being ridiculed, of people not understanding what I was trying to say, outweighed every advantage of taking the risk.

And so I spent class time pretending to be engrossed in work I didn't understand. During recess, I hid behind school pillars, fighting tears of shame, and wishing to God the ground would break open and swallow me whole. Home time brought little relief, given nostalgic memories of happy times and the dread of yet another day of irrelevance with no end in sight. The gnawing feeling that I didn't matter took over my life. I started hating myself. I sometimes wonder whether things would've been different had cell phones been around at the time. Maybe I could've hidden myself from my own self. Then again, maybe not.

That's when ED (the name I gave my eating disorder) showed up at my door. She crept in so sneakily that I never saw her coming. On a couple of occasions, I'd noticed some of the older girls at school looking at me with admiration. I wasn't sure what it was about until one of them said "*J'aime ta silhouette*" (I love your figure). With every identity snatched away from me, I grabbed for the one she'd tossed my way. Like a parched traveler, I lapped up the brief moment of attention. My dying soul had found a lifeline. And there was no way I was letting go of it.

I began controlling my food and skipping rope for an hour every afternoon. I pretended to finish my meals but fed them to the stray cats that lived behind our house. My parents wondered why I was losing weight and thought it was the stress of school-work. I didn't tell them the real reason. I didn't know the real reason. It wasn't about my weight or my body. It was about getting the praise and approval that made me feel I mattered—again. And before I knew it, the eating disorder had taken on a life of its own.

Decades later, I learned that when our sense of self-worth is inadequate, we depend on certain areas of our lives to feel good about ourselves. Dr. Jennifer Crocker, who researches self-esteem and self-worth at Ohio State University, calls these areas *contingencies of self-worth*. She has identified seven of them: family, performance (academic or work), appearance, approval, competition, God's love, and morality. They're usually tied to what was valued, rewarded, or criticized in our homes growing up, or in the societies we live in.

We *have* to excel in them because they are the yardsticks with which we measure our worth. No wonder, perfection isn't a choice.

For me, academic success and approval had both been contingencies. I kept putting in herculean efforts, as most of us do. But when the rewards stopped coming in Senegal, I felt stuck. Exposed. Desperate. And then I found a new contingency— appearance—and the rest is history.

More and more women and young girls are experiencing the same miserable stuck-ness I'd felt in Senegal. I've often seen clients turn to other domains of dependency when work performance begins to slip through their fingers. They try and control things at home, micromanaging their children or partners, who often become resentful or rebel against the sudden surge of input or advice. They change career paths or become a stay-at-home mom—all great decisions when they come from a place of optimal confidence. Or like me, they become obsessed with their appearance. It may not lead to an eating disorder, but it certainly leads to disordered eating.

I saw this play out during the pandemic in a way I hadn't expected. Women were forced to leave their jobs in huge numbers. Many of those who stayed weren't experiencing the wins that happen when the economy is in full swing and business is booming. Those who depended on work performance to feel good about themselves began spiraling down. Here's what a young man wrote to me:

> I know you don't work with men. But I was hoping you have some advice for me. My wife used to travel a lot for work, but now she's mostly working from home. This is affecting our entire family in a huge way. She's taking out her frustration on our three sons, and one of them is beginning to shut down. I'm not sure how to best navigate the situation, help my wife while at the same time safeguard the peace for the boys. I'm in a high -stress job myself, which makes it even harder. Can you suggest something that can help us through this tough time?

I was able to get his wife to sign up for a few coaching sessions. Sadly, I couldn't be of much help. Her almost narcissistic need for praise and adulation, which wasn't being met in the virtual workplace setting of the pandemic, had found a source of supply in her children's compliance and forced appreciation of her motherhood. She didn't think there was anything she needed to work on.

I never heard back from the family. It's my guess that given her kids were still young, they would continue with their praise and compliance for a few more years at least. By that time, she'd be fully back in the workplace, where she was quite adept at surrounding herself with people she could charm. My only hope is that if and when she's ready for change, it's not because she's lost the relationships that are near and dear to her.

The old saying "Wherever you go, there you are" is truer than ever for fragile confidence. Neither accolades nor praise, perfection, or success can soothe the pain of a hole in the heart. Understanding where this hole comes from (chapter 2) and how we can fill it (chapter 3) is the only way we can come home to our inherent worth. To our goodness and ability to create change. To the ground from which everything is possible.

The Origins of Confidence

It was toward the latter half of my recovery from the eating disorder that I began to notice what a prolific storyteller ED was. She loved to find scapegoats. If she could blame someone, anyone, or anything for my life, ironically even for the way I now looked, she could reign endlessly.

My treatment was initially inpatient, because I had to be tube-fed in order to monitor my electrolytes and make sure ED wasn't dictating what and how much I could eat. Once outpatient treatment began, I also had to meet with a therapist once a week to do the deeper work. I'd never been to therapy before and had no idea what to expect. All I knew was that I didn't want to be admitted again, because tube feeding had been a horrible experience.

It was during one of those very early sessions that my therapist threw me a curveball. I'd just told her that I'd thrown half my lunch in the garbage, and I figured she'd either express her disappointment or applaud me for having the courage to tell the truth. Instead, she looked at me with a very still face and, pulling the little notepad on her desk up close, inquired, "What's your relationship like with your mom?"

ED was seething that I'd broken my vow of secrecy, and while I tried to make sense of the therapist's question with my starved brain, she shoved me aside and grabbed the mic.

"She gets upset over everything," I found myself saying, even as I felt a twinge of guilt and my conscience tried to nudge me toward the truth.

"Tell me more," my therapist said, placing the eyeglasses that were hanging on a chain around her neck back on the tip of her nose. ED's eyes sparkled. She immediately came up with stories, some partial truths, some outright lies. And so began months of therapy sessions where ED turned molehills into mountains and spun yarns of falsehood around little nuggets of truth.

It wasn't long before I started believing the stories. The guilt transformed into toxicity, and my relationship with my mom, which had been quite close all my life, began to suffer. As a mother myself, I can now empathize with the suffering she went through during my illness. It was bad enough watching her only daughter wither away before her eyes. Now she also had to bear the pain of watching our relationship turn snarky, distant, and resentful.

Thankfully, my conscience gained strength as my weight crept up slowly, which it did, because it was the condition for staying outpatient. I began to see more of reality. I began to notice my mom's love and patience. I began to remember childhood days of cuddling together in bed late at night, after she and my dad returned home from an official dinner. And I began longing for the relationship that was critical for my recovery.

Over the years, I've seen much harm done on the premise that "everything that's wrong with you is because of your mother." It's a view that was commonly held by many therapists who were trained around the time the child–caregiver attachment theory came into being some fifty years ago. The theory highlights the importance of the emotional relationship between a child and her caregiver in the very early years of life and its impact on her later flourishing.

Attachment theory plays a central role in the development of optimal confidence because our earliest interactions are part of the implicit world. But it also places undue blame on mothers when things don't go well, because unlike those days, mothers are no longer the primary influence in a child's life. Even at the time, they may not have been for many of us. And if they were, there certainly have been many more influences since that have also imprinted themselves on your implicit world. Here are some to consider:

Multiple Caregivers

Since the women's liberation movement of the 1960s in the West—when women stepped into the workplace in increasing numbers—fathers, grandparents, nannies, and early childhood educators became equally if not more involved in a child's upbringing. The concept of caregiving shifted from a "primary" source to almost a web of influences that even go beyond human interaction. Almost all of us have turned to the television or the iPad in desperation when we struggle in that tight space between work and life. And the virtual world continues to impact us in subtle and not-so-subtle ways, given its the first thing we see in the morning and the last thing that tucks us into bed at night.

Personality

The impact of personality cannot be taken lightly, because nature and nurture feed off each other. As social psychologist Dr. Jonathan Haidt writes in his book *The Happiness Hypothesis*, "Children with sunny dispositions who have happy mothers are almost certain to play the game well."[12] It's far easier to raise a happy-go-lucky child than it is to raise a sensitive one, and women score higher on the personality trait of sensitivity. This can make little girls pick up on subtle signs of displeasure and feel responsible for it.

There's also the predominantly female personality trait of agreeableness that makes us more eager to please and avoid discord. Combine that with a caregiver(s) who rewards certain behaviors or is a little too eager in wishing the best for their child, and you have a pleaser and approval seeker in the making.

Sometimes, personalities can clash too—a highly expressive child can feel too much for a parent who needs time and space to themselves. Even similar personalities can clash; a child with panache may feel resentful of a parent who likes to hog all the limelight. When nature doesn't do a good job in the cards she deals out, there's a lot that gets dripped into the implicit world.

Circumstances

This one is so relevant to our lives today, where everyday pressures and stresses make it very hard to parent from a place of full presence and centeredness. When I think back to the time my twins were born, my heart goes out to the struggling me doing the best she could, given what I was dealing with. I'd had a nightmare of a pregnancy (that I talk about later in the book) and spent the last three months hospitalized and on bed rest. By the time the twins arrived, still preemies at thirty-four weeks, I was physically dystrophied and emotionally spent. As luck would have it, my father-in-law fell ill at the same time, and my in-laws moved in with us in our tiny downtown apartment. From being a comfortable three in the family, we were suddenly seven, including colicky babies, a vibrant five-year-old who'd been starved of my presence for three months, and two elders who needed constant care and support.

I'll never forget the endless days and sleepless nights when all I did was pump, feed, change, rock fussy babies, cook for the family, attend to my in-laws, scrape my depleted energy resources for my oldest, and cry tears of anger and desperation. I longed for some space, some time to myself, some help and appreciation. I longed for my old life. *Was this really the bliss I'd fought for?*

If I was less than the ideal mother my twins needed, it was because I was fighting to stay afloat. And I certainly wasn't the only one. Millions or perhaps billions of women go through similar challenges in a role they were never meant to do alone. It truly does take a village to raise a child, as the old proverb goes. But in today's world, where the stresses and struggles we face have skyrocketed and the social support we once had has plummeted, being the consistently present and attuned caregiver a child needs for her optimal emotional development is an almost impossible bar.

This is even more true in the aftermath of a pandemic that has thrown women's lives in disarray. In 2021, the *New York Times* ran a series highlighting women's struggles during the pandemic—working from home while educating their children, taking care of old and vulnerable parents, and not having the support system they once relied on to keep the wheels running. The article quoted a tweet that had 315K likes and was retweeted 66.5K times: "Am I working at my regular capacity? No. But am I prioritizing and taking care of the most important tasks? No. But am I at least taking care of myself and my mental health? Also no."[13]

Genes and Emotions

Emotional ups and downs are part of life, which is why we all have inhibitory neurotransmitters in the brain such as GABA (gamma-aminobutyric acid) that help us regulate the emotional transmission. Unfortunately, some of us are simply born with less of these neurotransmitters, and this can be obvious as early as age six. During adolescence, when the brain goes through a pruning and myelination process that sheds many of its initial neural networks, many young people can struggle to manage their emotions if they're left with less of the neurotransmitters than they need. Ironically, it's also a period when emotions are felt more strongly because the brain is undergoing a second learning spurt. This is one of the reasons most mood and psychological disorders begin in adolescence.

The research shows that intense emotions impact the implicit world because we're wired to remember them. It's based on the peak-end rule that states that our brains use mental shortcuts to organize our lives by what is emotionally salient (peak) and by how things end.

Bullies and Toxic People

The implicit world is also home to unprocessed emotions that are often a result of extremely upsetting experiences that exceed our capacity to make sense of them. Being bullied in school has a huge influence on a child's self-esteem later in life, and many little kids can change personality almost overnight.

Relationships later in life can also have a huge impact on how we relate to ourselves, especially intimate relationships, because they build upon the networks of child–caregiver relationships. These days, toxic workplace relationships can also dent our sense of self, because work is almost an extension of ourselves.

I remember Elise, who was a dog trainer with the police and whose job it was to track criminals and search the homes of suspects. She was young, had risen rapidly up the ranks, and won a couple of county awards for her role in heist arrests. Every time she shared the experiences she'd had, I would be in awe of her courage. But despite her competence and achievements, she had lost confidence in her abilities because of a new boss who was demeaning in how he spoke to her and belittled her when she struggled at some of the harder maneuvers. "I'm not the person I was," she said. "I now wonder whether I'm even good at what I do and whether I should be looking for something else."

Society

The impact of social systems, norms, and expectations on a woman's implicit world is so huge that we'll address it in detail in chapter 3 and again in chapter 6. But suffice to say, the framework we receive the moment we're born gets more and more demanding and obtrusive as we grow older, until it's a stranglehold of unreasonable and ambiguous expectations that speak to us in our own voice.

Little boys get a framework too, but save for the sensitive ones, they come through pretty unscathed because it's mostly aligned with their natural strengths and life aspirations. Take being single for example—women can experience a sense of worthlessness with it that men just don't. Research in women's studies shows that it's likely because women have been controlled through millennia by being told that their worth comes their relationships, and that their identity is defined by their partners. It has taken us forever to stop calling ourselves Mrs. (partner's name). And many of us continue to introduce ourselves in this manner.

Even the most secure childhood can lead to deep-seated insecurities, debilitating self-doubt, and ruthless self-criticism later in life thanks to society's unrelenting criticism.

MAKING SENSE

When clients come to me, they're usually trying to let go of behaviors that are getting in the way of their goals or happiness. One of the first things we do is talk about their early years, because of the undeniable role of childhood on the implicit world.

What has been a near constant in all these years of coaching is that most clients describe a childhood that wasn't traumatic or extremely distressing by any stretch of the imagination. I used to see a lot more of that in my previous life as a psychotherapist. But the women who come for coaching are largely in the nonclinical population. They're ambitious and have done well in their careers. They're raising families, dealing with stresses, and trying to manage it all in the best way possible.

When they revisit their early years, they talk about growing up in regular homes, with a mixed bunch of love and loss, joy and disappointment, praise and criticism. There are rarely deep scars that torment them on a daily basis. They're more like scrapes that haven't healed, because the brain looks for what matches its internal story. It's called *confirmation bias*; we keep scratching the wounds of our early years and keep the cinders of the past alive in our present-day lives.

Sometimes clients tear up as they talk about moments when they felt unseen or unloved. And sometimes there's hesitation too; as conscientious women, they feel guilty talking about their caregivers' behaviors, especially if they've passed on or are now supportive presences in their lives.

If you experience similar hesitation when reflecting on your own past, rest assured that the purpose is *not* to point fingers or place blame. Your caregivers were certainly not the only influence on your implicit world. Besides, they undoubtedly faced many challenges in raising you. Maybe they didn't have the support they needed. Maybe they were working overtime to put food on the table or in positions that left little time for parenting. Maybe they believed children should be left to their own devices and feared that too much attention would curtail their emotional development. Maybe they were tired or sick, caring for too many children, facing financial hardships, or unhappy in their relationship and together only for your sake. Or maybe they were carrying fears, limiting beliefs, and emotional baggage from their own past that transcends generations unless we do the hard and courageous work of visiting the inner world.

Regardless, the fact that you're here today, no doubt having faced countless challenges, having had multiple wins, and having shown up with the beauty of your heart more times than you realize, is also in large part due to your caregivers. **The aim of revisiting the past is to develop the awareness you need to take charge of your life**. As spiritual teacher and public speaker Anthony de Mello writes in his book *Awareness*,

"What you are aware of, you are in control of. What you are not aware of is in control of you."[14]

WHAT'S YOUR ATTACHMENT STYLE?

To help you make sense of your past, I'll lean heavily on the work of psychologist Mary Ainsworth, who played a key role in the development of the child–caregiver attachment theory. She classified mother–infant relationships into three distinct attachment styles based on a mother's emotional relationship with her child.[15] As you go over them, keep a couple of things in mind:

Think of all the factors above that may have influenced your implicit world, not just how your caregivers interacted with you.

The attachment styles below are extreme versions and mutually exclusive for the sake of classification. You'll likely fall somewhere in the messy middle.

To create her classifications, Ainsworth ran a series of experiments that she called *the strange situation procedures*. These experiments followed a sequence of events: the mother and infant enter a toy-filled room. They're then joined by a stranger. A few minutes later, the mother leaves, and the child is left with the stranger.

Then the stranger leaves, and the child is alone for a bit. Finally, the mother returns.

What determined the attachment style was *how the child responded when the mother returned*, not how much they cried when separated. This was to rule out the child's own temperament, because some children are simply more distressed by separation. My youngest daughter would bring the entire house down every time I'd drop her off at her Montessori. I literally had to tear myself away from her, only to go sob in my car, keep peeking from the windows until she was settled, and drive away carrying the guilt with me to work.

"I'M ENOUGH"

In the procedures, the infants who actively initiated engagement with the mother when she returned were classified as **securely attached**. They smiled, showed off their toys, or vocalized their joy in shrieks or funny sounds. My daughter would do a little victory dance that was as raucous as her morning distress. It was as though she was telling her little friends, "See, I told you she'll be back!" Her teacher would shake her head in amusement and say, "She's such an emotionally expressive child!"

It turned out that the mothers of the securely attached kids were attuned to their child's emotional needs and knew how to respond skillfully without becoming overwhelmed by their own emotions. Through their moment-to-moment interactions, the child was absorbing the sense that she was worthy of her mother's love and attention, regardless of whether she was "good" or not. According to humanistic psychologist Carl Rogers, this unconditional positive regard leads to self-acceptance, self-expression, and eventually self-actualization.

Think of it like the little child in the park who waddles off to play but keeps looking back to make sure mom or dad is still there. Or who's itching to climb the new jungle gym and needs just that nod of approval or a thumbs-up from her caregiver to go for it. When little children feel that someone they trust is watching over them, they are more courageous in their risk-taking, more confident in their decisions, and more resilient to knocks and setbacks, because they have a safe base to return to.

"I'M NOT ENOUGH"

Not all children reengaged their mothers in the experiments. Some continued to cry or angrily resisted the mother's attempts at comfort. Even if they quieted down, they appeared to be passive and clingy and unwilling to leave her side to play. Ainsworth classified them as **insecure anxious/resistant**. Their mothers were inconsistent in their reactions, warm and receptive one minute and tuned out, displeased, or worse, critical the next.

I remember a few years ago, sitting at the airport and waiting for my flight that had been delayed by many hours. There were quite a few parents with little infants on the same flight, and they were trying to skillfully respond to the needs of their tired kids. Some rocked and sang softly to their infants. Others walked their toddlers up and down the aisles or sat with them bleary-eyed in the play areas.

Sitting farther away, I saw a mother with three little children under the age of four or so. The youngest was buckled in his stroller, and the mother was trying to feed him. She would smile and make funny faces every time she approached him with a spoonful. She'd clap when he opened his mouth and pretend to chew voraciously when he tucked the bite away in one cheek. Every time he swallowed, I'd sense her relief in my body, because one of my twins had been quite a chipmunk when she was little.

But then I noticed how her interactions took an abrupt turn when he began resisting the food. Every time he'd dig his face sideways into the stroller or try and wiggle out of it, she'd plop him right back in, grind her teeth, and admonish him to sit still. I know she was exhausted, and I had flashbacks of my own frustrating attempts at feeding picky eaters. But then I noticed her older daughter standing on guard beside her. And my heart sank.

Her life seemed to revolve around making sure her mother was happy. She kept trying to urge her little brother to eat, even performing a little dance for him. She kept fixing her mom's scarf every time it slipped and would smile at her hesitantly when she was upset. Her little face wore her mother's emotions, and she seemed to have no desires of her own.

A child who grows up with anxious attachment believes she's the cause of her caregiver's unhappiness, because little children relate everything to their own selves. At the same time, she becomes hooked on the moments of love and laughter, because they make her feel secure. These on-again, off-again interactions do not nurture a safe base of self-worth; she feels she's not quite worthy of love and could always be doing *more* to get it.

She grows up to be clingy in her relationships and avoids risks because she's seeking approval and permission. As such, she never gets to fully explore or express what she really wants, and her pursuits are aimed at self-protection. Because of the occasional criticism, anxious attachment is more correlated with low confidence and impostor syndrome. Guilt, excessive conscientiousness, and emotional sensitivity are also common features, as are avoidant behaviors and discomfort with ambiguity and uncertainty. This limits growth and feeds back into the feelings of inadequacy and shame.

You'll likely relate with an anxious attachment style if growing up, you felt the need to walk on eggshells or manage the emotions of your caregiver or wanted desperately to keep them happy for whatever reason. Maybe you were rewarded for certain behaviors, even praised excessively for them, and criticized for others, even if it was subtle disapproval or in the form of advice. Or maybe it wasn't even how your caregivers interacted with you. There could've been problems in their relationship, financial or emotional struggles, or their reactions with a sibling who was particularly challenging for them. **Such experiences lead a little child to believe that love and approval go hand in hand and that self-worth is something you need to earn over and over again.**

"I'M NEVER ENOUGH"

The third attachment style that Ainsworth identified was **insecure avoidant**. These were children who showed no signs of joy when the mother returned; in fact, they ignored or otherwise actively avoided her. The mothers of these children were distant in their interactions and unattuned to their infants' needs. Strangely, they held them as much as the other mothers and took care of their physical needs. But they regularly rebuffed, even belittled their need for tender care. The children had learned to manage the pain of neglect by dismissing their needs; in their silence, they were telling their mothers, "I don't need you either."

The reality is that little children are constantly scanning their caregivers' faces to make sure they matter to them. It's a survival mechanism, because as helpless little beings, they rely on their caregivers for their physical and emotional needs. Do you see me? Will you be there for me? Will you care if I'm upset? When the children feel unseen regardless of what they do, the only way they can deal with the pain is by burying it beneath a sense of being more important or more capable than they are. Their core beliefs are as broken as their hearts—beliefs of superiority that mask a deep-seated sense of inferiority.

Individuals who grew up with avoidant attachment do not love themselves, even if they appear to be overly consumed by themselves. They're also emotionally unexpressive, distant in their relationships, and driven to prove themselves through their professional success—-the classic face of fragile confidence. Sometimes, albeit rarely, they *do* reach the top of the career ladder, if the profession they choose happens to be aligned with their natural strengths, if they face few hurdles to their advancement, and if they've totally turned the volume down on their emotions. These conditions aren't generally a part of a woman's internal or external experience.

I remember Megan, an experienced heart surgeon, who came to me because she was unhappy with her relationship with her brother. "I'm always the one who calls, and he rarely wants to talk anyway." Her reasons to fix the relationship seemed pragmatic: as a sibling, they needed to stay in touch. As we got talking about her childhood and early relationships, she spoke with the same head-centric approach as though she was describing someone else's life. "It was all normal. My mom was never around much and just critical about everything anyway," she said with a shrug. But then she began talking about her relationship with her brother, and her eyes welled up. "We used to have a lot of fun together," she said.

"You miss him?" I asked as she fought back her tears.

Silence. Then, "It's not like I'm needy or anything. If he doesn't care, he doesn't care. I guess I just need to accept that." Her relationship with her brother had been a bandage for the pain of being unseen and unappreciated by her mother. Now that he was married with three growing children of his own, his lack of time and attention was bringing up the pain all over again. And like before, she was trying not to feel it.

Think about it in your own life. Were you told to be strong or less sensitive when you revealed your softer sides? Was it all head and no heart at dinner conversations, all goals and achievement, and maybe even criticism of those who struggled or showed their vulnerabilities? Maybe you felt unnoticed growing up and sometimes just wished your caregivers had more time for you. Or more acceptance of your personality and more belief in your aspirations. Or maybe your family moved a lot and you regularly felt like an outsider, even if nobody ridiculed you or made you feel different. **Such experiences make a little child feel unseen or unwanted, and praise and success become the driving forces of their life.**

DIFFERENCE IN ATTACHMENT STYLES

	SECURE	ANXIOUS	AVOIDANT
Emotions	Emotional awareness and regulation	Anxiety and emotional overwhelm	Emotional disconnect/ numbing
Relationships	Healthy balance of give and take	Clinginess, giving at the expense of self	Distant, taking more than giving
Self-belief	Know and own strengths and aspirations	Undervalue abilities, comparison	Overestimate abilities, competition
Goals	Based on needs and values	Based on approval	Based on admiration
Journey	Perseverance and adaptability	Drifting with external feedback	Driven to prove self and unable to adapt

MASKING OURSELVES

An understanding of attachment styles serves an important purpose—it helps make sense of behaviors that seem otherwise incomprehensible, embarrassing, or perhaps shameful—the ones we keep shrouded in secrecy. When we understand that they exist for a reason, it brings a certain softness around them. A certain compassion for the little child who knew no better. And importantly, a certain distance that allows us to look them in the eye instead of justifying or denying them. It's the only way we can let go of the thoughts and behaviors that are getting in the way of our goals and aspirations.

In my research and experience, I've found that the two insecure attachment styles we've just addressed tend to have their own set of three overarching tendencies. I call them **masks**, because their purpose is to mask a perceived inadequacy or shame.

The six masks below (three in each of the two insecure attachment styles) are based on the three dimensions of core beliefs: our sense of self, others, and life. Of these three dimensions, "life" is more closely related to your area of contingency (from chapter 1); a mask of success can mean weight loss or a certain fitness level if the contingency is appearance. And it can look like a certain paycheck or position if it's work.

You may notice that a certain mask exists only in certain areas of your life and not the entirety of it. For example, you may be controlling at work, but you're pretty chill with how messy the kids keep their rooms. Or you may be a pleaser in your work relationships, but you have healthy intimate relationships where you can express your needs and desires.

There's the obvious reason that masks appear primarily in our contingencies of self-worth. But the other very important reason is that we exist in relation to the world around us. And given we've had so many influences on our implicit world, each situation may kindle a different genie from the past. **As you go over the six masks below, reflect on why and when a certain one tends to show up for you.**

"NOT ENOUGH"

Self: "I'm a good person."

Everything in your life is a ruling on your "goodness" as a person, whether it is being productive, helping someone, or ending your day a certain "right" way. Your greatest judge lives in your own head. And it's constantly analyzing your behaviors, measuring them against near impossible ideals, and pointing out where you failed—again.

Others: "I'm a nice person."

This mask is the pleasers, the appeasers, the givers, the over-apologizers, and the ones who cannot say no or set boundaries when needed of there's an inherent sense of inferiority. If you relate, you may also have experienced resentment, because the giving usually happens at the expense of your own needs. Or guilt, when it takes away time from the people who genuinely need you.

Life: "I'm competent."

You put in an insane amount of effort into whatever you do, because deep down, you undervalue your capabilities or underestimate your ability to deal with whatever happens. You compare yourself unfavorably to others, and your fear of failure or criticism is so great that you perfect and control so nothing slips through the cracks. Wherever possible, you avoid risks and play small. You likely realize all this—you may even be frustrated by it—but the fear of putting yourself out there is debilitating.

"NEVER ENOUGH"

Self: "I'm great."

This is the *superimposed* core belief of greatness that masks the pain of unworthiness. It comes with feelings of entitlement, a sense of superiority and self-righteousness, and ethical standards that can be quite fuzzy for yourself. This mask is difficult to recognize in yourself, but you'll know it's there if you have a tendency to show your smarts, to correct or criticize, or to judge others for their choices and decisions.

Others: "I'm strong."

A key feature of this mask is independence; and your life is designed with yourself in mind. You find it difficult to be emotionally vulnerable, and intimate relationships can be a challenge. You like to keep a certain "safe" distance, and even the natural needs of others can feel suffocating or too much. You also like to keep your challenges and fears to yourself because you don't want to come across as "weak" or "needy."

Life: "I'm successful."

You're driven by success and want to be noticed and praised for it. It's likely that your idea of success is closely tied to societal standards—money, power, possessions, fitness, beauty, being supermom, etc. Perfection is an underlying theme, but unlike anxious attachment, it is externally oriented (since you are already perfect). You want the perfect life, the perfect partner, the perfect kids who go to Ivy League schools, and perfect trips that are the envy of your friends. And you'll be loath to share imperfect parts of your life with others.

"BUT THAT'S WHO I AM"

When I talk with clients about how they may be hiding parts of themselves behind masks, there's a question that invariably comes up, especially toward the anxious attachment masks: How do I know it's a mask and not me being me? Just last night, Jillian, a senior manager at a nonprofit organization, said, "I'm not sure if I'm a people pleaser. My previous boss told me I was. But the one before that said I was a caring person and that she valued that in me. I think I'm a caring person. But maybe people take advantage of it? I don't know. It's confusing."

> "I need to work extra hard because I don't have a competent team/the right support/the highest qualifications."
> "I shouldn't ask for a raise, because people are losing jobs, and I'm lucky to at least have one."
> "I have to hide my tears/show myself to be strong, because that's the only way to get respect around here."
> "I can't say no to my boss, because she has been so supportive of me all along."
> Sometimes I also get an adamant, "I don't think it's a mask. It's what's needed in my work."

These concerns cannot simply be dismissed. After all, women often do have to leave parts of themselves at the door in order to do their best work. Besides, the expectations on them are higher as well, as they are for people of color. And then there's our own natures—we may be introverts or come alive when we're presenting, performing, or the center of attention.

So how are you to know when you're masking and when your behavior is situationally appropriate or an authentic expression of yourself? You cannot rely on your rational mind because cognition is fickle as we saw in chapter 1. It'll always come up with reasons to justify your behaviors as a way to calm the emotional discomfort of cognitive dissonance.

I believe the best way to tell the difference between a mask and authenticity is to reflect on how you *feel* when you engage in these behaviors. Do you experience a sense of ease, joy, and maybe a certain grace that comes from engaging your natural strengths and propensities? Or do you experience stress, an impending sense of disaster, or a desperate need to get what you want? What about letting go of the behavior if you know it isn't helpful? Have you tried and not been able to do so consistently? Does the very thought make you anxious? Rigidity is one of the key markers of a mask.

Authenticity (which is psychologically similar to optimal confidence) is flexible because we all have many self-identities. We're a paradox of opposing energies—we have both feminine and masculine traits, a cognitive side and an emotional one, a playful side and a spiritual one. As poet and journalist Walt Whitman wrote, "I am large, I contain multitudes."[16]

You can pivot to lesser used parts of your identity *without experiencing anxiety* because it doesn't expose something terrible about you. You can be collaborative in certain situations and assertive when the situation calls for it. You can be an introvert most days but tap into the more zestful and excitable parts of you when needed. You can be a helpful person in general but set boundaries with the colleague who dumps his work on you at the very last minute. And you can do so knowing he may not like you as much. Because that's okay. It doesn't shatter your sense of self. You'll also be able to do so *kindly*, because you're not trying to justify your actions or prove why *you* are in the right.

"BUT THAT'S WHO I WANT TO BE"

I couldn't end this chapter without addressing the other, somewhat related confusion: "What if I *want* to be like that?" "What if I'm okay with the hard work because reaching the top of my career makes me feel good?" "What if being a giver makes me feel like I'm living a good life?" "What if being conscious of what I eat makes me feel I'm respecting the body I've been given?"

These are also genuine concerns, because we want to feel we're making the most of the life we've been given. We want to do work that makes an impact. We want to belong to others and touch people's hearts. More than anything, we want to grow into the best version of ourselves in service of the roles and relationships that matter to us. This is the inherent need to self-actualize that is louder today than ever before.

The confusion arises because of the societies we live in. Every day, we're pulled away from who we are to who we are expected to be. Some of it is a normal part of being a social animal—we do need to adapt to the world around us. But how are we to know when our goals are based on our values and self-expression, and when they are a reflection of the voices we've grown up and live with?

Again, it comes down to the *feeling* that Anthony de Mello describes as the difference between "soul feeling" and "world feeling." You'll know the difference when you offer a genuine apology as opposed to an attempt to appease. You'll know it when you have a heartfelt desire to make a difference, and when your efforts are about wanting to be on the cover of *Time* magazine or to have ten thousand followers on your Insta account.

There's nothing wrong with fame or a following. I know I would love both. But when they are the drivers of our goals, we are *extrinsically* motivated. The journey is ridden with anxiety, comparison, and burnout. And success—if achieved—feels unfulfilling because it was never what we truly wanted.

Goodbye, Perfect is about identifying your *intrinsic* aspirations, because optimal confidence connects you to your soul's longings. Perfection is not a goal, but an aspiration. It's a North Star that guides you, but that you never quite reach. The journey of self-actualization is like an asymptote; every day and until the very end, you keep moving closer and closer to the woman you came here to be.

Chapter 3

The Journey of Optimal Confidence

Very early in my research, it was clear to me that by what we value and reward in our homes, workplaces, and societies, we've been building fragile confidence all along, and the main beneficiaries have been men—primarily white men—at the expense of all minorities. Corporate America's vows to be more inclusive, especially after a pandemic that disproportionately sidelined women and people of color, have borne little fruit. Competent and conscientious marginalized groups, the ones we desperately need at the helms of our workplaces and societies, are barely represented at the highest levels. In fact, studies show that the better credentialed a woman is, the more her income and career stagnates.[17]

Something is terribly wrong.

I believe that one of the major contributors to this stuckness is our approach to helping women and minorities advance into leadership roles. Without an understanding of what confidence is and how it develops and plays out in our lives, **we're trying to solve our problems with the same approach that created them**. Instead of focusing on what's missing—empowered *implicit* beliefs—we've been strengthening the explicit ones.

It's no wonder that there's little to show for the time, effort, and money invested in women's leadership development over the past decade. The needle toward gender parity at the top has budged ever so slightly, and the recruitment and retention of women in STEM professions continues to be challenging despite the efforts and incentives involved. This has far-reaching effects. Without equal access to some of the highest-paying professions and positions, women are facing a "feminization" of poverty that will affect them and their families for generations to come.

A different approach is urgently needed. It's needed so women realize their full potential and experience the fulfillment that comes from it. It's needed so we can make steady progress toward equitable and thriving workplaces and societies. And it's needed so we stop feeding the downward spiral of a misguided approach. When efforts at leadership development don't meet women where they are, there's cynicism and loss of trust. Some women blame themselves for not gaining from the programs, feeding the underlying belief *something's wrong with me.*

The few who do make it to the top find that they twisted themselves in such convoluted ways to get there that they long for the person they once were. They may not even recall that person. But the feelings of emptiness tell them they lost something precious on the way. There are regrets, more guilt, more depression. They wonder whether the sacrifices to their health and relationships were worth it. And many times, they feel it's too late to do something about it.

A TOP-DOWN APPROACH

Our current world, its institutions, structures, and ways of knowing, have been built on what is commonly called a *patriarchal approach*. Patriarchy is a loaded term and can stir up a lot of anger and resentment in many of us. So let me explain what it means in the context of our lives and leadership so we can be more effective in our efforts toward women's advancement.

A patriarchal approach is based on what Plato described as an "ascending directionality" toward an actualized life.[18] It's one that places "masculine" forces such as intellect, rationalism, and an enlightened vision at the helm of our decision-making. These forces exist in all of us regardless of gender. So do "feminine" forces such as intuition, connection, and conversation with the deepest parts of our individuality. They take the "descending directionality" of a matriarchal approach.

As writer and speaker Fabiana Fondevila writes in her book *Where Wonder Lives*, the two directionalities complement and complete each other.[19] We're meant to flow between them, to seek silence, a slight distance from the noise of the world, then return with renewed energy and engage in the world from a place of empathy and compassion. Or to experience something in the real world, an outrageous act or one that inspires us to turn inward to make sense of it, so we know what it's calling us to do.

However, with the advent of modernity and especially the age of reason, all forms of feminine knowing came to be sidelined, even rejected. The wisdom of our inner world—of ancestors and traditions, the dialogue with our fears and desires, our dreams and intuition—was considered a lesser intelligence. Rationalism became the new divinity, and everything else was either superstition, weak, or ungainly. This thinking naturally became the dominant force in workplaces, made by men and for men.

It also affected societies as a whole by creating a top-down approach to right and wrong. Certain feelings and fears were discouraged, if not outright forbidden, leading to what author Robert Augustus Masters has called "spiritual bypassing."[20] It's when we endure repression by others in the name of being closer to a higher power. Or we repress or avoid our real experience or self-expression because it's deemed wrong, illicit, or "unspiritual."

For women in particular, it has felt like a one-two punch. Take anger for example, because it's a huge one for women. From very early on in our lives, we're trained to suppress angry emotions. Even as little girls, we're rewarded for not making a big deal of things or letting go of our stance so others can get their way.

As we grow older and become aware of the unfair ways of the world, we become angry. And, yes, women are angry. In fact, we're enraged, and rightly so. But because society tells us we cannot be angry, many of us are turning the anger inward and becoming depressed. Those who do speak up are criticized; multiple studies show that anger in men raises their profile. For women, there's no end of denunciation that comes with it.

The reality is that it's almost impossible to right the wrongs in our lives and in the world when we don't have access to our anger. In a recent *Sunday Paper*, the weekly newsletter written by author and journalist Maria Shriver, the topic was the social changes brought about by angry women. "Rosa Parks was angry. Harriet Tubman was angry. Mother Teresa was angry (yes, she was). Many of my she-heroes were and are angry, and thank God they were."[21]

To express our righteous anger in effective ways (because suppressed anger will spew out and cause more harm than good), we have to first learn to befriend it. Because we cannot transcend something, we never had a grasp of in the first place.

THE FUTILITY OF FIXING

A top-down approach is *prescriptive*, where problems are to be "fixed," not befriended. We have what award-winning author Jeremy Lent describes as a "mechanistic view of nature."[22] It's about how things *should* be, without a full understanding of the way things are.

When fixing doesn't happen the way we want it to happen, we can become enraged and hopeless, neither of which is helpful. Or we distract ourselves (and there's no end of distractions) and start living with a hood over our heads, oblivious to the suffering and to our responsibility toward it. This is starkly evident in our world today where we're seeing either rage, criticism, and division over the challenges we're facing or an apathy that's incomprehensible given we're driving ourselves to hell in a handbasket.

Fixing may have worked in another era, when problems were less complex, the world was less uncertain and volatile, and a few people at the top did have all the answers. But given the complexity and deep roots of our challenges, in a world where billions of people have answers that feel right for them, and where what's right today may change by the time we wake up tomorrow, fixing is leading to silos and division and making misfits of the very people we desperately need in the midst of our creative processes and decision-making.

I see this all the time in my work. Just last week, a young woman called me to inquire about coaching sessions. I was instantly drawn to her soft tone, her thoughtful responses, and that oh-so-slight shyness. "I'm a strategy and operations manager at [one of the big four tech companies]," she said. "It's always been my dream job, and I worked hard for it. But I feel I should be looking elsewhere." She went on to explain how the people she worked with were "should we say mostly a type A personality," and she was finding it difficult to do her best work in the midst of all the competing egos.

It is also placing undue stress on leaders whose only tools are the ones that created the problems in the first place. As a result, we're seeing a lot of unhelpful and ultimately unproductive patterns of behavior, such as risk aversion, frenetic and short-sighted activity, and stubbornness, control, and loss of trust. Professor and researcher Erik de Haan, who has been coaching leaders on working through change for over two decades, states that a leader's natural strengths can become "overcooked" in the face of extreme challenges.[23] He writes about the need for mindful reflection, compassion, and insight, all elements of a matriarchal approach to leadership. **Because without the feminine, the masculine becomes tyrannical in nature.**

A BOTTOM-UP APPROACH

"All serious daring starts from within," wrote novelist and photographer Eudora Welty.[24] The challenges in our world are calling for daring in our homes, workplaces, and communities. They are calling us to be the heroes we've been waiting for, because we're our only hope. But before we step into the role that's being asked of us, we have to understand what it means to be a hero in today's world.

Today's hero is not Superwoman who flies in to fix what's not working because fixing itself is not working. It's the person who is actively involved in the struggles of marriage and parenthood, of work and community, of justice and equity *within her circle of influence.* In her book *Who Do We Choose to Be?*, writer and speaker Margaret Wheatley calls these circles our "islands of sanity."[25] They are small spheres where we're committed to bringing about positive change through the matriarchal qualities of acceptance and compassion, valuing the truth of interconnectedness, and being grounded in the vibrant and dynamic flow of life.

This bottom-up approach will also pick up where the first two feminist movements left off. Even though the fight was for women's rights and led to progress in women's advancement, it left behind women of color, who did not have access to the same privileges as white women. Currently, minority women, which includes Black, Asian, and Hispanic women, are in the boardrooms of just about

6 percent of Fortune 500 companies. At the current rate, most women of color will not see their proportional representation in boardrooms in their career life span.

In her book *A Decolonial Feminism*, Françoise Vergès writes of those earlier movements: "They believe patriarchy to be worse than racism, capitalism, and imperialism. Obviously, they don't take into account the fact that colonialism cemented the patriarchy."[26] Women were playing on a man's playing field, where the rules were patriarchal and they had to *prove* themselves to be just as capable and deserving as men, and then some. The fact that we're back to fighting some of those same fights, about abortion, equal pay, and equal caregiving work, shows that we were standing on shaky ground.

It's now time to create a new playing field. To uproot systems that favor any one group over another. To embrace intersectionality. To change the rules of the game. To create ways of being, knowing, and learning that honor the feminine face of human nature and the deepest truth of our common humanity. Only then can we harness our anger, frustration, and hopes toward real and lasting social change.

AN UNDERLYING WISDOM

I've often noticed how things or events that appear completely unrelated seem to have a meaningful connection. My research in optimal confidence and my interest in societal systems had no apparent connection. In fact, the two didn't even take place at the same time. But then I started noticing similarities. Like Plato's approaches to life, confidence too has two models of formation and formulation.[27] There is the outside in model, where our confidence comes from the external world. And then there's the inside out model that begins up close, in the very fiber of our being.

Much like the approaches to life, both models complement each other. A sense of goodness allows us to be vulnerable in our relationships, and the feedback from the relationships, even if it is in the form of more joy or feelings of trust, feeds back into our sense of goodness. Similarly, trusting that we have qualities and abilities that matter allows us to take risks and go after opportunities, and the feedback, whether success or failure, builds the sense that we can deal with whatever comes our way.

And again, much like the approaches to life, the work always begins within because the explicit (feedback and conscious thoughts) makes it back to the implicit world only if the stories are aligned. Research shows that when feedback doesn't match how we feel about ourselves, we're unlikely to agree with what others say, even though we may agree with the same feedback about someone else.[28] It doesn't feel right somewhere deep inside.

I began wondering if these connections were pointing to a larger wisdom. I began noticing the similarities with nature, and trees in particular because they are the oldest living organisms around. The growth and resilience of a tree depends on the strength of the roots that support it. Yes, you still provide it with the right external conditions once the seedling sprouts. But unless you've nurtured the seed, unless you've tended and tilled the soil, you can water it all you want and still end up with a struggling tree.

Whether it's the seeds we grow, the societies we create, or the confidence we build, we cannot forget an underlying wisdom: flourishing is bottom-up, starting way within.

For too long, we've focused primarily on skills such as collaboration, assertiveness, productivity, and risk-taking as a way to build women's confidence. All these are important. But without their corresponding implicit components, they're either disjointed efforts or the same top-down approach that's building fragile confidence and leaving women exactly where they are: stuck.

Women are trying harder, getting more and more educated, and massing more and more proof of their competence. But despite it all, they're experiencing the same gut-wrenching self-doubt every time they need to step outside their comfort zone. They're comparing and competing, because their worth is measured by their ability to come out on top. And in any scarcity-driven competition, sooner or later, they won't be at the top. What happens when failing isn't an option? They try harder from a place of lack—or lower their standards to meet a wavering sense of self-worth.

There was a time in our collective journey when self-worth didn't matter as much because our aspirations were less lofty. But in our day and age, when the longing to become everything we're born to be is as urgent as the need to be so, optimizing our confidence isn't a choice. It is the call of the moment.

UNDERSTANDING OPTIMAL CONFIDENCE

The research defined optimal confidence as a psychological construct comprising of two sequential components: **belonging and mastery**. Belonging precedes mastery because safety in a relationship is essential for speaking up, taking risks and thus developing the sense that we can deal with whatever comes our way. As such, attachment style directly impacts belonging, and by consequence, mastery as well.

In anxious attachment, both belonging and mastery are suboptimal. We're desperate to be liked and thus do not take the risks that can help us grow. Avoidant attachment, on the other hand, lacks belonging, but mastery *can* be possible because we're eager to prove ourselves. It's not a given though, because the hurdles are many and the pressure can be crippling. Even if it were to happen, it's devoid of joy because belonging is intrinsic to a woman's sense of fulfillment.

Since the components of belonging and mastery are implicit, they need a little explaining to be fully understood. Belonging is different from reflected appraisals and feedback because they represent our conscious perception of how we're viewed by others. **It's more intuitive and can best be experienced as an inner sense of security when we're around others**. Secure attachment provides this inner sense of security, which then generalizes to other people and makes us feel safe in our relationships. My clients often admit to having a supportive boss or team they're working with. But they still struggle to voice their ideas or ask for what they need. In fact, without a felt sense of belonging, the support they receive can become a source of dismay; they blame themselves for their stagnation, and this certainly doesn't work wonders for their confidence.

The same applies to mastery. We often confuse mastery with competence, even though it's a much broader construct. Mastery isn't about being on the dean's list or being the youngest senior-level manager at the firm. Nor is it about having great credentials in a certain niche or the best expertise at a certain task. **It's about trusting our instinctive desires and having the courage to learn and grow in the pursuit of what feels intrinsically rewarding.**

Think of it as a child making sandcastles on the beach. There's no self-evaluation involved. There's no inner critic telling her that her sandcastle looks like it's about to fall or that it doesn't measure up to her older sister's perfect one. There's simply the joy of being engaged in what she loves, the courage to put her ideas into practice, and the openness to feedback from the very act of creating.

This deep passion and engagement can certainly lead to competence and proficiency. But starting out with building competence does nothing for true confidence when we have implicit beliefs to the contrary.

THE JOURNEY AHEAD

My research gave me a thorough understanding of optimal confidence: where it came from and what it comprised of. But it did not provide a tested framework to build it, given the implicit world is inaccessible to conscious intervention. I had to find my own way.

It occurred to me that optimal confidence develops organically when a child grows up with secure attachment. What if we were to establish the key characteristics of optimal confidence as our milestones, and retake that childhood journey?

It sounded promising. The research on habit formation shows that it is far easier to let go of a bad habit when we *replace* it with an empowering one.[29] To me, it's like walking through a trail. You take a certain route every single day and the grass stops growing beneath your footprints. You cannot grow it back by forcing the blades to stand up. But you can ease it into regrowth by taking a different route.

We experienced this as little kids in Sri Lanka. My dad was deeply invested in our education, and since we were homeschooled, he decided that we do the Singapore curriculum given its rigor and excellence. I was in grade four and my older brother was in grade six—and both of us struggled initially. Our private tutors tried to help by working on what we were doing incorrectly, and we simply ended up more confused and more behind.

That's when my dad decided that we needed to start all the way back from grade one. Our basic approach and assumptions were incorrect. And trying to patchwork over them was both painful and perilous, much like building a castle on shaky ground. Both my brother and I flew through the younger grades in less than six months. But the difference we experienced was one I remember to this day. For one, it was joyful. Everything made sense because it built on what came before. It was also affirming—we never felt "wrong" or stupid for being confused or incorrect. And most of all, it was empowering. We could put our learning into practice and actually see results.

That is the experience I wanted for the confidence journey. Because the implicit world is not only about our fears and misguided beliefs. **It is also the magical home of our gifts,**

our dreams, desires and unmet potential. Why would we *ever* turn a blind eye to that? And why would be keep arguing with ourselves, disproving and challenging unhelpful thoughts, or trying to convince ourselves of why we are as good or capable when we know it doesn't work? Isn't it time for a more uplifting, more vibrant, more *true* journey?

In the chapters that follow in part 2, we'll be journeying through the four key characteristics of optimal confidence in the following order:

1. Feelings of self-worth
2. Trusting and supportive relationships
3. Authenticity and purpose
4. Courage and resilience

In the process, we'll build each of the two components of confidence (belonging and mastery) first from the inside out and then from the outside in. For women in particular, confidence is a two-way journey.

> This layered and bottom-up work will give you the safe base to be vulnerable in your relationships, the curiosity to explore your potential and self-expression, and the courage to go after your dreams knowing full well that

you will face challenges, failures, and criticism along the way. Slowly but surely, you'll build that magnetic quality we call true confidence: the trust that you're good and deserving, and that you have what it takes to figure things out even through the mess and mistakes.

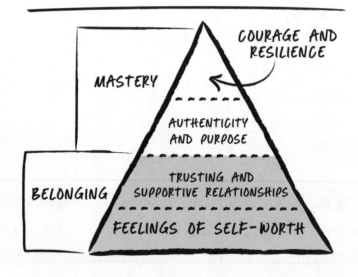

THE CONFIDENCE JOURNEY

COURAGE AND RESILIENCE

MASTERY

AUTHENTICITY AND PURPOSE

BELONGING

TRUSTING AND SUPPORTIVE RELATIONSHIPS

FEELINGS OF SELF-WORTH

Please engage with the practices in each chapter because we know from the science of neuroplasticity that we can mold our brains through our actions. Neurons that fire together, wire together. **What we do is who we become.**

The more you practice, the easier it'll get, I promise. Slowly but surely, you'll begin to see yourself differently. It's like when you see the "other" image in an optical illusion. It takes a while for it to fully take hold. You keep drifting between the old and the new, wondering whether you lost it. Until one day, you'll realize you've finally become her. Finally come home to yourself.

MOTHERING OURSELVES

A key element of the journey you're about to take is the mental creation of a secure attachment figure for each of the four components of confidence. It is based on the principle of *potentiality* that Aristotle described as the possibility that lies within each living organism and *actualizes* if the conditions are right. You may also know it by its less technical term *entelechy*, defined in the German Idealism movement as the force that propels us toward self-actualization. Both philosophies affirm that this possibility lies in the acorn just as much as it lies in all of us. We each enter the world carrying something unique that wants to be lived out through us. And the extent to which it does depends on that something receiving the right conditions.

If you've seen a Bonsai tree, you'll know what I mean. Planting the seed in a tiny container, keeping it away from sunlight, and pruning its growth every so often results in its perfectly tiny size. A child who grows up with insecure attachment is the human version of the Bonsai tree. Perfect perhaps. But alas, stunted in her psychological growth.

Unlike other species, human babies arrive in the world highly dependent on their mothers. Thanks to our evolutionary transition from walking on all fours to walking upright and the narrowing of the birth canal that came with it, we're born "uncooked." We depend on our mothers not only for our physical needs, but also for our psychological growth because the integration of the brain happens best when a child feels loved and seen by her caregiver.

Nature wires women with nurturing qualities so they bring out the best in a child. When these qualities are expressed, as happens in secure attachment, the child learns to relate to herself with the same compassion and nurturance. And when they are not to varying degrees, or when the reassuring voice of the caregiver gets drowned out by the criticisms and demands of a world that wants to fashion us in its own image, we have our work cut out for us.

And as women, we almost always do. Most of us do not, cannot, will not give ourselves the same understanding we're so willing to give others. We turn away from ourselves every time we face setbacks or failure, the very times we need ourselves the most. And we refuse to celebrate our successes, believe in our dreams, and high five ourselves along the way. **We've ingested the patriarchy we grew up with and live in, and it now speaks to us in our own voice.**

The inner mother is the warm and loving presence who helps us live through dark nights of the soul and the dumpster fires of many days when we don't have our sh*t together. She's the one who reminds us of what's important and helps us stay open to life and generous in our beliefs about people. She encourages us when we dream big and paves the way when we wander because she has the same fire in her belly for our dreams as we do. And yes, she's the cheerleader who waves to us from the stands and reminds us to be playful, feel inspired, defend ourselves when needed, and laugh at ourselves when we take ourselves a little too seriously.

Maybe most of all, your inner mother is the ultimate confrontation with yourself so that every time you fall from grace, you befriend some new part of yourself that reminds you of the woman you really are, and have always been.

GOODBYE, PERFECT

This book is based on the simple premise that we cannot say goodbye to perfection, pleasing, proving, or any other unhelpful behavior *unless* we also build empowering implicit beliefs of confidence. Most of us have tried without lasting success. We've tried to be easier on ourselves or let go of perfection, but it's just ended up being more work. We've tried setting boundaries, being less judgmental or maintaining a sense of calm, but ended up doing quite the opposite.

This is because our behaviors serve a purpose. They protect us from judgment, real or perceived, and help us feel seen and loved, two fundamental needs of the human psyche. Unless we build trust in the beauty of our hearts and the brilliance in our souls, we cannot show up in the world without them. It's neither possible, except with grueling effort, nor wise, because we'll be tampering with the innate ability to protect ourselves from harm and hurt.

I experienced this in a weirdly interesting way during my eating disorder recovery. Around the time of "extreme hunger" when I was eating well over four thousand calories a day, I was mortified to find that my hair started falling out in bunches. *What was happening?* This wasn't something I'd foreseen, and I began to panic. "I think I'm eating too much," I said to my therapist. "I'll have no hair left if I continue like this."

She explained that the period I was going through was one of deep repair. My body was finally trusting me to feed it and initiating all the essential work that had been neglected in order to keep me alive. Now that it was ready to grow new and healthy hair, it was shedding the old and brittle hair that had stayed on simply to protect me from the cold that my starved body could barely tolerate, and from the knocks and bruises I may not have had the energy to heal.

It's the same with our unhelpful behaviors. The stronger our sense of confidence, the easier it'll be for the outdated parts of our personalities to fall off on their own or with a gentle tug, because they're not burdened with the responsibility to protect a fragile ego.

The hundreds of women who have been through the Goodbye Perfect journey have experienced transformative shifts in their lives. They've found freedom from their fears and ways to work through them that are generative, not more of the same. They've learned how to take feedback in stride and unhook not just from criticism but also from praise, because it's a product of the same shame. And they're engaged in work that's uplifting and impactful, because our heartfelt desires always include joy and connection.

I wish the same for you, dear reader. I hope that as you go through the book, you'll experience the freedom that comes from embracing the sweet core of your being and owning the life that longs to be lived through you. That is true confidence—your greatest gift to yourself, and to the world.

Let's begin!

Part 2

Building a Sense of Belonging

Chapter 4

Belonging to Yourself

You know that pit of shame or disgust you fall into when you say something you wish to God you hadn't said? Or when you do something that doesn't quite align with the person you like to think you are or how you want others to see you? It doesn't have to be anything huge. Maybe that prickly comment on parenting hurt your sister, or you made a few snide remarks about your colleague's promotion. And now you feel icky and terrible and wish the ground would swallow you whole. At least for a while.

This feeling isn't limited to social interactions. You can feel angry, ashamed, or disgusted with yourself for not fitting into last year's dress or for not ticking off all the items on your to-do list.

Or because you're out of dog food again, *and* you've been feeding the kids frozen pizza for the past three nights.

In fragile confidence, *anything* can become a judgment of our worth if it is related to our areas of contingency. For me, parenting has been a key contingency ever since I became a mother. If I'm not as loving, understanding, and encouraging as I'd like to be, or if my children are not as conscientious and responsible as I'd like them to be, I can be really hard on myself.

Being a perfect mom was so much easier when they were little because little kids generally don't test you as much. You feed them, you clothe them, and you provide enough opportunities for them to laugh and play, and life is pretty okay.

As they get older, rebellion, mood swings and messy rooms make it far more difficult to feel great about our parenting all the time. For me, those not so proud moments were not so pretty—I would spiral down into a cacophony of shame and blame.

I can't say the downward spiral doesn't happen anymore. It does, though far less frequently. More importantly, I have learned how to get out of it in a way that builds my worth instead of diminishing it. Take last month for example. My twins were home from college for the weekend. Having both of them home at the same time doesn't happen that often, now that social lives are back to what they used to be pre-pandemic. So I wanted their visit to be truly special.

It was the night before they were leaving, and I was alone in the kitchen. I'd insisted on doing the cleanup by myself because, well, it's easier. Plus, I wanted them to watch the basketball game on TV together, the way we used to do during lockdown.

The cleanup took longer than I'd expected, and because no one came to check in on me, feelings of resentment did. The happy sounds from the family room didn't help either. *Shouldn't they have come to at least ask if they could help? Life does seem all fun and games when someone else is doing all the dirty work. I'm too nice, and they take advantage of it.*

Had I been more centered in the moment, I would've recognized my distorted thinking and taken my thoughts less seriously. I may have noticed the exaggerations or dismissed them as absurd. I may have popped my head out the kitchen door and called them in to help. But in hindsight, the banter outside had stoked the painful memory of fun and laughter coming from the playground as the thirteen-year-old me stood alone under the staircase in my school in Senegal. The painful feeling of not mattering overpowered me.

My breath quickened, and my heart raced. My thoughts raced faster: *They'll take and take and take and it's all my stupid fault. They'll go enjoy their perfect lives, and I'll be left miserable and all alone.* My head spun. A surge of energy rushed through my body. I yanked the gloves off my hands, and before I knew it, I'd burst out of the kitchen like a raging bull and was unleashing my emotions all over them.

The details are thankfully a blur. I vaguely remember the children staring back at me in shock. I think they tried to defend themselves, but there was no way I was letting them speak. I yelled over them, making little sense, even to myself. My head begged me to stop. It told me I was being unreasonable, that I would regret it later. It kept reminding me that I wouldn't be seeing the twins again for a while. But my body seemed to have a mind of its own. The mind of a lunatic, if I'm being completely honest.

It took all of me to drag myself away to my bedroom and shut the door behind me. I wish it ended there. But no! I kept flinging the door open to spew some more nonsense until it was all out. That's when the energy suddenly gave way to exhaustion. I crumpled into a heap in the middle of the room, blame and anger now stewing with shame and remorse in a salty broth of tears.

The voice in my head that had egged me on in the kitchen suddenly changed course. *What's wrong with you? What mother behaves like that? And you go around giving your clients advice? If only they could see you right now!* Then, with an air of finality, *You've destroyed everything. They'll always remember this. They'll never want to visit again.*

That last jab left me sobbing uncontrollably and feeling disgusted with myself.

GUILT, SHAME, AND DISGUST

I wish that when we fall into that dark and scary place of *What did*

I just do?, we could look ourselves in the eye and say *It's okay, sweetheart, it happens! You're feeling terrible right now, let me give you a hug. And then we'll wipe those tears and figure out what to do.* Sometimes we do do that, but it's usually in areas that are not a self-worth contingency.

But when we depend on an area to feel good about ourselves, we cannot give ourselves permission to be imperfect. Instead of feeling guilty about what we did, we feel ashamed of ourselves. Guilt and shame are both "self-conscious" moral emotions that helped our hunter–gatherer ancestors stay loyal to their tribes and thus ensure they weren't left alone to face the dangers of the wild or of competing tribes.

Guilt is somewhat different from shame though, because it's associated with a behavior and thus fixable. There's a sense of agency involved. Shame, on the other hand, is when you're criticized for being defective as a person (*You're mean* vs. *What you said was mean*). There's little you can do about a flaw in your basic human design, hence the action tendency is to shut down. It helped our ancestors show remorse, in the hope that others would feel sorry for them and take them back into the safety of the tribe.

In our everyday lives, guilt is when you lie awake at night wishing you could take back what you said to your friend in a moment of anger and call them the next day to apologize. Shame is when you start avoiding them altogether. Guilt opens the door for analysis and amends. Shame shuts it tight and turns off the lights.

In their research on shame, Dr. Linda Hartling and her colleagues at the Stone Center at Wellesley have identified three common reactions to shame that they call *strategies of disconnection*:[30]

1. **Move away**: withdraw, silence yourself, start avoiding people and/or situations
2. **Move toward:** please, appease, go out of your way to make sure others don't dislike you
3. **Move against:** blame, shame others, make sure people know it wasn't your fault

In fragile confidence, the shame response has a fourth reaction as well that I call **move up**. It is the tendency to raise the bar higher for ourselves in order to feel better about ourselves. The presentation didn't go so well? The next one will be way out of the ballpark. Made a fool of yourself at a social gathering? You'll be the epitome of grace and dignity at the next one.

This dual action tendency to run away from what's bad and run toward what's good symbolizes the emotion of disgust.[31] Disgust was one of the very first emotions to evolve as a way to keep animals safe from contaminated foods and surfaces. It's why you gag or throw up at the sight of certain foods or why you wash your hands after touching raw meat. You're distancing yourself from what's dirty and may harm you and purifying yourself at the same time.

When humans began banding together, disgust also became an "other-condemning" moral emotion to help our ancestors distance themselves from those whose behaviors disgusted them, because it meant they couldn't be trusted. And to align themselves with those who they considered good and right because that's where they felt safe.

Disgust shows up as a "self-condemning" emotion in fragile confidence because the unworthy and the perfect are both within us. And when we do something wrong, or think we have done something wrong, we have no choice but to raise the bar even higher on ourselves. **It's like abandoning and punishing ourselves at the same time.**

That night, I'd hit rock bottom again, that deep place inside where the pain of unworthiness still hurts. And perhaps always will to some extent. And again, I heard the voice, still alive, still unrelenting: *Go appease them. Justify your behaviors. Blame your editors and the tight deadlines. And make sure it never ever happens again.*

How I was to make sure of it, I had no idea. There was no path to becoming better. But that wasn't important in the moment. The thought of being the perfect mom—of never getting upset, of never even feeling upset perhaps—made me feel better about myself. And that band-aid was enough for shame.

THE INTERNAL FAMILY

When I was in the throes of my eating disorder, I obeyed ED without a whimper because I didn't realize a fear-driven part of me had taken control of the mic. *Weigh your cereal when no one's watching. Throw out the lasagna in the garage bin. No one ever checks there. Break up the fish fillet into small pieces and slip them one at a time into your lap. Mom won't even notice. And never mind the smell in your clothes.*

I never questioned a thing. And ED rewarded me well for my obedience. She reminded me how light my stomach felt and made me believe emaciation was the same as emancipation. She noticed the regular fat on every healthy girl and reassured me I was a "better person" for not having it. The celebration was always short-lived though. ED kept me hungry, and not just literally. Invariably, she pointed out something more I should've done, something less I should've eaten. The plans for the next meal were always more stringent, the exercise always more exhausting. If I experienced any sense of joy, ease, or satisfaction in my life, I was obviously on the wrong track.

When I absolutely couldn't obey her wishes, either because all eyes were on me as I withered into nothingness or because my inner demon (that was ED's name for hunger) took over me, she would lose it. She would look at me in disgust and bathe me in shame. I still remember some of her words. *Animal. Out of control.*

Stupid. Spineless. There was imagery too that made me feel like garbage. And with that, she'd threaten to leave.

Of course I'd beg her to stay. She'd convinced me that without her, I'd be fat, ugly, and lonely. She needed promises that I'd try harder. That I'd commit to a day of starving to make up for the splurge. Or an hour of skipping rope out in the sun. I hated skipping rope; it would make my soles bleed. But ED didn't like compromises. It was her way or the highway.

I share this because we all have our own EDs, our own shame-based voices that are trying to hide a *perceived* inadequacy or unworthiness from the world by making sure we meet certain standards they believe to be essential for our survival. I say "perceived" because they are based on the interpretations of the limited awareness of our early years. And I've found that one of the best ways to separate ourselves from them is through an understanding of the internal family systems approach.

This approach was developed by Dr. Richard Schwartz in the 1980s as a way to help clients with mental health disorders, including anxiety, depression, substance abuse, and eating disorders. At the heart of the approach is the belief that the mind is naturally multiple, with three overarching parts, each of which serves a healthy purpose when it's in balance with other parts. When we suffer, get stuck, or lose direction, it's because we lack an overarching "Self" to keep the parts in check. Before we understand the

Self better, let's see how the imbalance of parts plays out in our lives:

Exiles are the inner child that carries both pain or fear from the past but also our sources of joy, passion, and wholesome inspiration. When in balance, exiles are a reminder of where we need to heal and grow, a guide to our callings and purpose, and the gateway to an actualized life. When out of balance, exiles become engulfed in fear and shame, and our gifts and dreams stay hidden and unrecognized because the two "protector parts" take charge of our choices and decisions.

Managers are one of these protector parts whose role is to make sure the fear or pain from the past doesn't flood our conscious awareness so we can carry on with our social obligations.. When in balance, managers help us get out of bed when we have no motivation and make sure we stay accountable to ourselves and to our roles and responsibilities. When out of balance, they become pushy, don't take no for an answer, engage in social comparison, keep wanting more from us, and become the source of stress and burnout. Here's how an unchecked manager can sound: *Why didn't she like my post? Maybe she doesn't like me?* Or *"I haven't done much all morning, I'm so, so behind!"* Or *"What if my presentation isn't as good as the last one. I'm freaking out!"*

Firefighters are the other protector part whose task is to help us learn from our past. When in balance, firefighters guide us toward the right decision when we're impulsive and trigger healthy guilt, remorse, or regret when we make mistakes, so we make repairs where needed. When out of balance, they prevent us from expressing ourselves or going after our dreams and shame us when we say, do, or even feel something that isn't aligned with our ideals of perfection. When shame is high, they may also push us toward numbing behaviors like overeating, drug use, or overwork.

"PROTECTOR" VOICES

I've often thought that managers and firefighters—when out of balance—are like a fearful and hurting older sibling who is desperately trying to protect a fearful or hurting younger one from the criticism or neglect of a caregiver who doesn't approve of her. Depending on her experiences, this older sibling can be loud, forceful, convincing, critical, demeaning, hopeless or any combination of the above.

Most of us experience her as the inner critic. But she also shows up as the inner victor/inner victim combo that Brené Brown describes as "the false dichotomy of victim or Viking."[32]

The **inner critic**

This is the voice that is often mean and rude, but can also pretend to be on your side, which makes it difficult to recognize. We'll be doing a lot of the recognition work in chapters 6 and 7, but for now, it's helpful to know why the inner critic is so prevalent in women's lives.

There is of course the impact of attachment style. Anxious attachment gifts us with an unrelenting inner judge, who can also be mean and harsh if we grow up with criticism.

There is also the criticism we ingest from a society that holds a very high bar for women. Even workplaces hold women to higher standards as compared to men. And research also shows that the *kind* of criticism women receive is mostly personal, related to who we are as opposed to what we did.

There are other factors too. Biologically, we're wired to be more critical of ourselves; any oversight on the part of a hunter-gatherer mother could've meant death for her helpless little one. We're also more consciousness because women have traditionally been in charge of taking care of others. Thus we've developed a more vocal inner critic that makes sure we perform our roles well.

And finally, there's personality, the undeniable impact of our genetic makeup. Those of us who are more sensitive are not only more clued in to other people's signals and emotions, we can also be harder on ourselves when these are negative. All in all, we tend to be the ruminators, the ones who question whether we did the right thing, and then beat down on ourselves because more likely than not, our answer is that we didn't.

The **inner victor / inner victim**

This dichotomy is common in avoidant attachment because of

the dual core beliefs of superiority and inferiority. When things are going well, the voice is of the inner victor who self-glorifies, corrects others, even puts them down. **We judge others to feel better about ourselves.**

When things don't go as well, it's the inner victim who blames, seeks sympathy, refuses to take responsibility, and can become quite hopeless and depressed. These are typical behaviors of fragile confidence that are documented in the scientific literature.

For reasons we saw earlier, this combination isn't commonly seen in women's lives, especially as the inner victor. Neither our society nor our personality allows us to be so pompous about ourselves, and thankfully so. Humility is a wonderful quality if we don't mistake it for putting ourselves down to make others feel better.

Even our inner victim tends to morph into the inner critic at some point because of a high conscience. Once we've spread the blame around, we start thinking of how we may have been unreasonable or how others have it much worse. We think of the whales that are dying and the current economic system that is tearing the world apart. And we start feeling lousy for having made such a big deal of something ever so minor in the scheme of things. Enter the inner critic.

THE EMOTIONAL LANDSCAPE

In the internal family systems approach, the Self is characterized by the eight Cs of compassion, curiosity, calm, clarity, creativity, courage, confidence, and connectedness.

These qualities emerge organically through secure attachment where caregivers are **present, attuned, and nonjudgmental** of our inner world. This helps us build awareness around our emotions, be present with our joys and upsets, and respond from a place of higher consciousness, instead of reacting with our more primal instincts.

In fragile confidence, the Self is underdeveloped for obvious reasons. Depending on our early experiences, we become disconnected with our emotions or hooked by them because little children make sense of their emotions through their caregivers' reactions to them.

UNABLE TO FEEL

In avoidant attachment, caregivers are not fully present or attuned to a child's emotions because of their distant emotional style. This compromises the development of *bilateral neural connection* between emotional and reasoning capacities in the child's brain. As she grows older, she'll find it difficult to know when she's in distress, and even if she does, she'll take a head-centric approach to her distress (pop a pill, go to the gym, etc.) instead of trying to understand what she really needs.

A few years ago, during the brief economy bust, Rebekah

approached me at a particularly stressful period in her life. She shared how tense she felt with deadlines at work, her "highly critical" mom's upcoming visit, and the closing on a house that she felt was just right for her.

"I want you to take special care of yourself at this time," I said. "Everything depends on your health and well-being." She said she'd been very disciplined about going to the gym. "And what about checking in with your body and listening to what it wants?" I asked.

Rebekah smiled. "I think I'm okay," she said. "I just need to get through this week. There are two important deliverables at work, and I cannot mess up."

Two days before the closing on the house, she called me in tears. "I called the whole thing off. I just couldn't do it. My back gave way, and I'm on bed rest. I don't even know what I want anymore. I feel lost."

Rebekah later told me how, as a little girl, her mother would tell her to "go out and play" or "have a snack" when she was upset about a hurt at school. As an adult, her self-care routine was pretty much what was touted by wellness industries, which benefits them way more than it benefits us. True self-care is so much more than manicures or a gym membership, although it can certainly include that. It's about being present to our body's signals because our bodies speak to us through emotions and subtle feelings. When we don't listen, they find other ways to get their needs met. Rebekah's back giving way was no coincidence.

In its extreme form, an inability to feel shows up as not knowing when to stop or give ourselves a break, nor knowing when our creative juices are calling us to go full throttle. We're also disconnected with the outer world because both these worlds are interconnected. We experience little empathy, no real joy, and no sense of being alive. We're like machines, and every day is the same.

LEARNING TO FEEL

Here are two simple practices that you can start incorporating in your life if getting in touch with your body has been a challenge for you.

Body scans are like a walk through your physical body. You start from your toes, and as you shine the light of your awareness on each part of your body all the way to your shoulders, jaw, and temples, they come alive. And the more you feel the sensations, the knots, or the restlessness, the more you can have a conversation with them.

The other practice is one I learned from Dr. Daniel Siegel's work on interpersonal neurobiology.[33] It's about *describing* an event in your day, either in a diary or to a friend. People with underdeveloped bilateral neural wiring find it easy to talk about facts *(she was already late when she came, so we left for dinner immediately)*, but struggle to describe feelings, body language, and subtle nuances *(she looked flustered when she came and my heart jumped a beat*). *That* is what builds neural connection between your emotions and reasoning.

UNABLE TO BE

In anxious attachment, the caregiver's inability to be fully present or attuned to their child's emotional state is because they struggle to manage their own emotions. This impairs the development of *vertical neural connection* between emotions and the prefrontal cortex, the seat of conscious processing.

Imagine a little child going to Mom or Dad with a physical or emotional hurt. And imagine them reacting with:

"Oh my God, oh my God, what happened?"

"Stop crying, I can't deal with this!"

"This shouldn't have happened; you'll never be able to get over this!"

"I feel really scared. What if..." It's now the *child's* job to soothe the caregiver.

Sometimes it isn't what they say, but how they say it. The shock, pain or fear on a caregiver's face is enough to overwhelm a child.

When a caregiver magnifies, suppresses, or fixes a child's emotions, they will run roughshod over her all her life. So will other people's emotions, because she doesn't learn to separate self and other. She too will run around with her hair on fire, needing others to be happy or to keep their emotions in check so she feels emotionally stable.

I remember this one time when my twin daughter came home, threw her bag on the couch, and slumped down at the kitchen table where I was getting lunch ready. I could see she was upset and instantly rushed to the rescue: "What's wrong, honey? Tell me. Is it your friends? Did the teacher say something? It's okay if you got a bad grade."

It turned out she'd had a fight with her bestie at school, and her pain cut right through me. I barely let her finish talking before I launched into a barrage of solutions, offering strategy after strategy on how to feel better, even going as far as to share the scientific backing for it.

Suddenly, the lifeless figure before me sprang off the chair and darted up the stairs, screaming, "You always do this. You never listen. You don't even understand!" I was this close to running after her, half of me wanting to appease her, the other half fuming at her outburst and ingratitude. Luckily, wisdom prevailed (plus the quesadillas in the oven needed attention). Once I was calmer, I could remind myself that she wasn't looking to be rescued. She simply needed me to *be* with her in understanding. Once she was calmer, she'd figure out what to do.

When we don't learn to be okay with not being okay, we can also resort to numbing behaviors to ease the emotional surge. And these days, there are plenty to choose from: drugs and drinking yes, but also excessive busyness, shopping, Netflix, bingeing, mindless scrolling through our social feeds...

LEARNING TO BE

This practice will help with vertical neural integration because it creates space between your emotions and reactions. And that space will help you access the brain's seat of conscious processing.

When you feel the emotional surge, you need to name the emotion(s) as accurately as possible. In his book *Permission to Feel*, research psychologist Marc Brackett talks about the importance of widening our emotional language. Unless we know exactly what we're feeling, we can't give ourselves exactly what we need. And that causes more frustration, more offloading of emotions, and more misguided action.

Our emotions are like little children. Sometimes just naming them makes them feel seen and calms them down. And when we need to do more, we're doing what's needed, and not shooting in the dark.

There are other ways of being with your emotions scattered throughout the book. The most common is the breath—as psychiatrist Victor Frankl said, it creates the space from which we find "our power to choose our response."[34]

There's also self-compassion and the inner compassion presence that we'll create later in the chapter. And then there's the Riding the Wave practice that we'll unpack in chapter 7. It's my absolute favorite for emotions that are so strong that they're accompanied by impulsive behaviors.

THE HUMAN CONDITION

Being present and attuned to our emotions is one thing. They are two of the three essential qualities of a secure attachment figure. But what if you lack the third quality: nonjudgment. What if you judge yourself for the way your feel? This isn't uncommon at all—judgment and criticism usually come with the territory of insecure attachment. Even secure attachment walks us out into a world that is judgmental and critical.

Last week, a woman reached out to see if I could help her with her habit of comparing herself to other women. "When I see a woman who is happier, it brings me down," she wrote. "I am already practicing gratitude, and a friend told me I should watch movies about those who are less fortunate."

On our call, I asked her if she could allow herself to feel what she felt. She was aghast. "Isn't that terrible?! I mean, jealousy isn't a nice emotion, is it? I don't want to be jealous. I want to feel happy for other people. But it's hard, and I feel like a bad person."

If it's not jealousy, it's anger, worry, resentment, regret, or unhappiness. We all have emotions we try to deny or distance because we've been told they're bad or wrong in some way. Maybe you grew up with, "We don't do anger in this house," or "Keep a cheerful face. I don't like unhappy people," or, like my client, "Jealousy is for the mean-spirited." Maybe you were punished for it or constantly preached about the sins of your follies.

When I was growing up, there was this happy-go-lucky cousin who was the bane of my existence. Nothing seemed to bother her, and she had this way of laughing out loud that, quite honestly, irritated me a little. I was different. I was more sensitive, less excitable, and had been told that I was an "old soul". It wasn't meant as a compliment.

"Why can't you be more like your cousin" was a phrase I heard so often it could've been tattooed on my head. I'd even tried, but it had been draining, and I'd felt seriously fake. The more people told me to be happy, the more I began hating the H word.

It became worse when I started my studies in positive psychology. "You study happiness" became the new guidepost. Its stake would be driven into the ground the minute I expressed my upset or frustration over something, however valid the emotion. Never mind the myth that positive psychology is the study of happiness. It's not; it's the study of flourishing. And never mind the fact that flourishing begins with the nonjudgmental acceptance of the entirety of the emotional landscape.

About a year into the pandemic, when the world was engulfed in death and despair, Brené Brown interviewed psychologist Dr. Susan David on her podcast *Unlocking Us*. The two spoke about "toxic positivity," the belief that despite pain or difficulty, people should always exude a positive outlook, and how it was adding to the pain and suffering caused by the pandemic. The incessant memes and posts on "the bright side" were making people feel weak and defective for feeling unhappy.

Toxic positivity also has a twin: comparative suffering. Comparative suffering is when we compare our suffering to that of another who has it worse in order to get away from our emotions. The problem in doing so, the research shows, is that we're tallying our overlooked blessings as a sort of penance, because we feel guilty for feeling the way we do.

During the pandemic, when my four adult-ish children and I were locked down in a two-bedroom apartment for what seemed like an eternity, their round-the-clock complaints reached a whole new level. Someone's too loud. The sun is too strong. The professor is a farce. The stupid chair has broken their back. Now they need special attire. And Amazon only delivers after two days. Urgh!

I couldn't deal with their negativity, especially given I was dealing with my own fears about the future. I tried to be patient, but bottling my emotions simply led to frequent blowups and the misery of now having to clean up their mess. In desperation, I turned to gratitude, even though I knew it had lost its charm on them. When they were little and mommy's words actually meant something, gratitude worked wonders. Their little eyes would sparkle as though I'd thrown them a lifeline. As they got older, they started rolling their eyes every time I uttered the G word. During the pandemic, they outright begged me to stop. "All I want is your empathy, Mom," my daughter said in exasperation the day she found out in-person college had been delayed by yet another semester. I was midway through telling her, "It could be so much worse."

And it wasn't just me. Many of my clients couldn't talk about the trials and tribulations of homeschooling, about being bummed that their favorite coffee shop was closing down, or about feeling deeply upset that they wouldn't get to see their grandchild's firsts without adding "I'm so grateful we're safe." I would tell them what I was struggling to accept myself: **It's okay to feel what you feel.** Losses are meant to be grieved, disappointments soothed, longings nurtured.

When we judge our feelings, we not only add salt to our wounds, we also never get to know what they want of us. Because feelings come from that part of us that wants to be expressed through us. For the woman who had reached out to me, jealousy was a call to explore what she truly wanted to do with her life. And for my children, the negativity was a reminder of what they valued, and to connect with the people they missed.

There honestly is nothing wrong with worry, jealousy, anger, or any other "negative" emotion. It doesn't mean we give ourselves permission to act on all emotions. That's where the Self comes in. Her role is to listen without judgment, so we can call on better angels of our nature.

PERMISSION TO BE HUMAN

In her beautiful poem "A Brave and Starting Truth", the poet Maya Angelou writes:

> *"Out of such chaos, of such contradiction*
> *We learn that we are neither devils nor divines."*[35]

Perfection is not for us mere mortals. We exist in that space of in-between construed in the Renaissance conception of "man" and illustrated by artists of the era. In their paintings, you'll find adults above animals and children, and below angels, gods, and goddesses.

It isn't just the arts or philosophy that have wondered about who we are as human beings. In his scientific research on moral emotions, Dr. Jonathan Haidt explains that the vertical dimension of Divinity is essential to how we see ourselves in our social space.[36] At its two extremes are the emotion of disgust, and the sublime emotions of awe, love, humility, and connectedness. We rise and slip on its vertical pole.

Being human means that invariably we'll make mistakes and misjudgments. It means we'll do the thing we swore we'd never do, or *not* do the thing we promised we would and end up disappointing someone dear. And it means we'll feel horrible about it because we aspire for the divine in us and we fell short of our ideals.

"There is no such thing as bad people. We're all people who sometimes do bad things," writes Colleen Hoover in It Ends with Us.[37] And when we do, we *will* experience shame, because it's one of the few primary emotions that's equally distributed across the population (unlike happiness or fear, where some people are naturally wired to feel more of it). In fact, *not* experiencing shame is far worse, because it says something about our ability to feel remorse.

So what do we do when we find ourselves in that pit of shame or disgust? The research on compassionate focused therapy shows that self-compassion is the antidote to shame and disgust because it embraces the very brokenness we want to hide from ourselves and others.[38] Unless we hold a loving space for our thoughts and feelings, however appalling, and forgive ourselves for our mistakes, however bad, we cannot grow into better versions of ourselves.

Nor can we grow collectively; when our hearts are so hardened against ourselves, they cannot extend for anyone nor let anyone else in. "Love yourself. Then forget it. Then, love the world," wrote beloved poet Mary Oliver in her poem "To Begin With, the Sweet Grass."[39] Of all the qualities of the Self, compassion for ourselves is the most fundamental, the one that gives rise to all else.

THE MAGIC OF SELF-COMPASSION

One of the saddest parts of doing the self-compassion work with clients is that many of them feel undeserving of it. *How can I be kind to myself when I thought a horrible thought/ate an entire box of cookies/didn't finish my work on time?* They believe they have to earn love by doing something that makes them worthy of it.

They may look at me like a little child seeking permission. "You're sure? It feels weird. No one ever spoke to me like that." Some tear up; they talk of times from their past when they wanted someone to notice them, understand them or be nice to them, but no one did. I remember one client talking about her struggles with weight. "My dad would get really upset if I took a second helping and would tell my mother to stop me. I would feel really humiliated, so I started eating when no one could see me. I still do that and then feel disgusted with myself."

There are countless similar stories. How they felt unseen when a baby sibling arrived. How they were always compared to that "perfect" someone. How they did everything to get attention from a dad who was the life of every party but never made them feel special. It's heartbreaking to think of the exiled little child who's stuck in the past, hungry for love but feeling unworthy of it.

Almost always, there's also the client who thinks self-compassion is weak or will get in the way of her success. She'll say something like, "I know me. I have to push myself. Otherwise, I'll become lazy." Or "I'm in a high stakes profession, I can't possibly be all soft and easy with myself." Dr. Kristen Neff, who studies self-compassion, has found that *weak* and *demotivating* are two common myths of self-compassion.

However, countless studies show that self-compassion is a far better motivator of change than self-criticism, because it leads to greater perspective and courageous action. It also leads to less procrastination or performance anxiety, more openness to risk and opportunities, and greater loyalty and team cohesion.

This is because being kind and understanding of ourselves shifts us from the *threat* mode of the sympathetic nervous system (where we're on high alert to signs of danger) to the parasympathetic system, where we feel naturally calm, compassionate, and connected to our higher capacities for reasoning and perspective. This is solid ground from which we can see nuance, appreciate other points of view, and connect to our values and a vision of who we want to be in the world. We can then engage the *drive* mode of the sympathetic nervous system to take a courageous stand for what we need and value.

Paul Gilbert, who received the Order of the British Empire for his work in mental health care and is the founder of the Compassionate Mind Foundation, calls it the difference between *secure and insecure striving.*

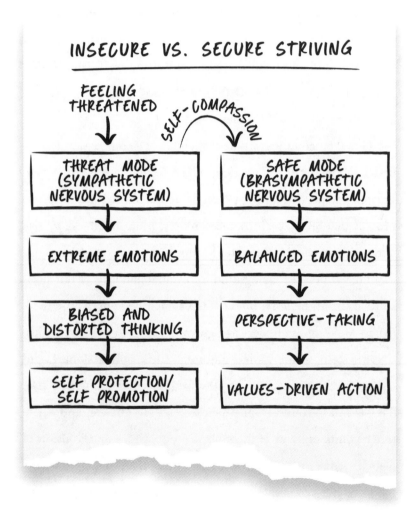

INSECURE VS. SECURE STRIVING

FEELING THREATENED

SELF-COMPASSION

THREAT MODE (SYMPATHETIC NERVOUS SYSTEM)	SAFE MODE (BRASYMPATHETIC NERVOUS SYSTEM)
EXTREME EMOTIONS	BALANCED EMOTIONS
BIASED AND DISTORTED THINKING	PERSPECTIVE-TAKING
SELF PROTECTION/ SELF PROMOTION	VALUES-DRIVEN ACTION

The good news is that compassion and courage are part of our evolutionary inheritance. Mother or not, we have maternal instincts of care that are tender but also brave, because nature has wired us to be "mama bears" when the situation calls for it. The challenge is that these instincts are biologically directed toward *others*, and life experiences have directed them *away from ourselves*.

The internal family systems approach works so well because the "self" we know is the fearful part of us that needs distancing, while the "other" is the exiled part that needs nurturing. The more we turn toward her with unconditional love and acceptance, the more our true self will emerge in her unique and glorious expression.

THE INNER COMPASSION

To relate to yourself with the love and compassion that is your birthright, you have to first create an inner presence that exudes the qualities of warmth, wisdom and nonjudgment.

Begin by imagining what she looks like. There is no right or wrong way to do this, but the more detailed you are in your visualization, the more you'll feel her presence in your life.

I've had clients imagine everyone from Mother Mary to Grandmother Willow, the spiritual talking tree in the Disney movie *Pocahontas*. Some think of their dog or another pet, or even a teddy bear or doll that was part of their pretend play lives. A grandparent is a common one; less so is a parent, but it can certainly be, especially if your relationship deepened as you became older.

The image can also be a mix of many people, fictional and real, or a place or a moment in your life that feels or felt safe and comforting. Maybe, it's being in nature or playing an instrument. One of my clients would bring to mind her "blankie" from when she was little. Another called her presence "tea with Grandma" because it reminded her of the happy times when she would visit her grandmother in the country. **Regardless of who or what your presence looks like, it needs to make you feel loved and accepted just the way you are.**

You also need to give your presence a soft and comforting voice. Research on the polyvagal theory highlights the importance of tone in strengthening the vagal nerve and shifting us from the threat response to the parasympathetic response.[40] Touch is important too. Placing both hands on the heart like an embrace releases oxytocin and calms anxiety. If your fear is on high alert and you find yourself shutting down, place one or both hands on the tummy with gentle pressure, because that's where the first branch of the polyvagal nerve begins. It's associated with the freeze response.

Here are some questions that will help you bring your inner compassion to mind when you need her the most. Because that's when your inner protector parts will be at their loudest, and wouldn't let you think:

> How does she relate to you when you're feeling down? Does she hug you, stroke your arm or your hair?
>
> How does she calm you down when you're anxious or overwhelmed? What does she say to you?
>
> How does she help you find the bigger version of you when you're feeling small, silenced, or sidelined?

Your inner compassion can be specific to a certain area of your life, where you carry deeper fears or shame. You can also have many versions of her, because you may be bringing a different set of fears or beliefs to different areas of your life.

LEARNING TO LOVE

Once you've created your inner compassion, make her an integral part of your life. Walk and talk as though this loving presence is living through you. Every day, maybe multiple times a day, look at yourself in the mirror, and with your hand firmly on your heart, say "I love you." Say "I love you, sweet child." Say "I love you, precious soul." Say whatever you would say to someone you love dearly.

I have tried it myself, and all I can say is that you have to do it to experience it for yourself. The very act of looking at ourselves feels vulnerable. We normally ignore ourselves in the mirror, sometimes purposefully so. Or we get hung up on things we don't like—the sagging jawline or droopy breasts, the dark circles around our eyes, and never mind the fact that we were up past midnight finishing up something important.

All the while, there's an inner child who wants to be seen and acknowledged. She wants to be told she's loved and that she won't be alone. So essential is this need to be seen and loved that nature locked it into the very physiology of feeding through the release of oxytocin, the "love hormone." It's what creates those priceless moments when mother and child are locked in mutual eye gazing. In the rise and fall of each breath, the mother's silent wonder, and the child's fixation with her face, the child is seeking her own soul. She is learning to fall in love with herself.

I remember how one of my twins (my little girl) would refuse to drink milk when I was tense or distracted for some reason. I'd try to hide my stress by smiling and pretending to be fully present. But she would read my internal signals and look away, as though deeply hurt I wasn't giving her what she needed. She needed to see her soul in my eyes. And my eyes weren't truthful enough for her to do so.

As you look at yourself in the mirror, look for the beauty of your soul. Look past your jowls and your wrinkles, past your thoughts about what you'll be doing today or regrets about what you should've done differently. Look at yourself like the mother and child, or like spellbound lovers on the French Riviera. Because who you see before you is someone who deserves nothing but your utter and outright infatuation. You're a miracle, a force unto itself. To come alive, you need the loving gaze of your own attention.

LEARNING TO FORGIVE

I knew Anna as a member of the Goodbye Perfect Program. She had three grown boys, one of whom did not want to talk to her, and her pain was palpable every time she spoke. She said she felt guilty that she hadn't provided him with the time and understanding he needed when he was little. He'd been diagnosed with ADHD as a child, and she hadn't taken his diagnosis seriously. "People told me doctors overmedicate children, and I hoped he'd learn to focus as he got older. I know he felt ignored. I was a bad mother. He doesn't even want to talk to me anymore."

One day, she said, "I want to cry. I think I'll feel better if I cry it all out. But the tears don't come. I feel like a stone." My heart hurt for her. I knew she was exceedingly hard on herself. Sure, there were things she could've done differently. But hey, who gets this impossible parenting thing right, anyway? She was now trying to make repairs for the past, and it was unfortunate that her son wasn't ready to engage with her efforts.

Anna had already done the inner compassion work and was good about bringing her presence to mind when she recognized she was being hard on herself. But many times, she wasn't aware of the subtle ways her inner critic was eating her up. So when she spoke about wanting to cry, I asked her to start a daily practice of looking at herself in the mirror, placing her hand on her heart, and saying, "I love you." I'd read about the practice in Dr. Shauna Shapiro's beautiful book *Good Morning, I Love You*.[41] In it, she shares her own emotional downpour and how the practice released her shame around her failed marriage.

Anna appeared eager, but I didn't see her at subsequent coaching sessions, and I began to worry. Was she okay? Was she too depressed to attend the calls?

Then I got an email. I've pasted it below, because only her words can do justice to her experience:

Homaira, the practice has changed my life. I felt guilty doing it at first, as though I wasn't taking responsibility for the past. My inner critic was loud, and sometimes it was hard to look at myself in the mirror. But I was desperate and kept trying because you'd told me it could take a while. Then one day the tears came. First a few, then lots and lots of them. I don't know what I saw in the mirror that day, but it was someone beautiful. I wanted to touch this person I saw and without knowing it, I was saying "I'm so sorry. I'm so sorry." Maybe I was saying it to my son, but I know I was saying it to myself as well. I don't know how long I cried, but I feel a ton lighter. I feel at peace. And I feel that if I keep doing the right thing, our relationship will get better. I really believe that. I can't thank you enough. You came into my life when I needed you the most. May God bless you. Anna.

If you carry shame around an aspect of your life—perhaps a failed marriage or business venture, perhaps your body or a child who is unhappy with their life, perhaps a certain attitude toward certain people that you wish you hadn't had—try the practice and see if it works for you.

Especially try it out if there are parts of you that elicit shame in you. Researchers Tamara Ferguson, Heidi Eyre, and Michael Ashbaker call them our "unwanted identities"—parts of us we want no one to see, including ourselves. They are the exiles in our internal family.[42]

For me, "ill" is a huge unwanted identity. To this day, my instant reaction to a physical ailment tends to be *Is it my fault?* And to feel a huge sense of relief if I find there was nothing I could've done to prevent it. Even so, I struggle to give myself the rest I need to recover, or to ask for more time or understanding from others.

We all have unwanted identities, and given their origins, we've likely tormented ourselves for years so they stay out of sight. When we become aware of this, we need to hear an apology from our protector parts for the pain, stress, overwhelm and suffering they caused us.

APOLOGIZING TO OURSELVES

Anna's apology to herself reminded me of the years that followed my eating disorder. Even though the days of deprivation were behind me, I found myself hooked by anger and resentment. *Why did ED have to enter my life? Why had my adolescence been spent counting calories while everyone else experienced their firsts—their first kiss, first love, first trip alone, first apartment and job. How was I to just pick the pieces up and move on as if nothing had happened?*

One day it occurred to me that I really needed ED to say sorry for the pain she'd put me through. I dismissed the thought at first, because it sounded bizarre. But my mind kept going back to it. Something inside insisted on a sincere apology. How I was to do it, I wasn't sure.

And then one morning, it just happened. I got out of bed, picked up my journal, and wrote down the date. It was March 8, 1989. I began writing a letter: "Dear sweet child..." An hour later, I penned off: "I'm sincerely sorry. ED."

In that hour, I apologized to the innocent child I was, for

depriving her of an adolescence, for the lost years and the relationships that were affected. I apologized for the words I had used, for the lies, the half-truths, the pushing, the tormenting. And I swore that I will never hurt myself again. It was draining. But it brought me the closure I needed.

To this day, I've continued the apology practice, albeit without a letter. When I feel I've been wrongly hard on myself, when I've driven myself to tears or burnout, when I've denied myself rest or the right to be human, I put my hand on my heart and say sorry. "I'm sorry, my love, for forgetting about you." And I tell myself what I will do differently so I take care of this precious being inside.

I think this is so important in our world today where we can do everything right and still end up with a lien on the house or adult kids living in the basement and wonder where we went wrong. We can have the best intentions but then offload our stress and frustrations on others and feel even worse about ourselves.

It's okay. It's human. But it's *not* okay to simply move on without letting ourselves know we'll be more understanding of ourselves the next time around. Sometimes, we *really* need to hear that from ourselves, just like we really need to hear a sincere apology from others when they harm us in some way.

An apology from others builds trust in the relationship. An apology from ourselves builds the trust that we'll be there for ourselves.

R.I.S.E

I'm sharing a framework I created for those of us who need a step-by-step process to climb out of the pit of shame when we're beating down on ourselves for a mistake, a weakness, a flaw, or an imperfection. You can also use it for fears, frustrations, regrets, resentment, and feelings of guilt.

It is particularly helpful in the initial days of inner compassion work, because the neural pathways of self-compassion will still be in their infancy. When the firefighter is shouting at full volume and scurrying back and forth across your mental jumbotron, you'll need something tangible to manage the chaos and meet shame with compassion. The acronym, **RISE**, makes it easy to remember, because it's about rising above the emotional and mental clamor and choosing to be on your own side.

Restore calm by bringing your inner compassion to mind. This is about being *present* with yourself, the first of the three requisites in a securely attached relationship. If you feel an urge to run away from the unease or pain, breathe from your belly, and say something comforting to yourself like *It's okay love, I'm here.* If the inner critic is loud, let it know you've got things under control. Hug yourself if that feels good, or stroke your arm, or rock yourself lightly. Do it for as long as it takes to feel calmer and more centered.

Inquire about your feelings and what you need. This is

the second requisite, that of being *attuned* with your inner world. These questions can help:

What am I feeling?

What am I fearing?

Where does it hurt?

Where does the hurt come from?

What will help me right now?

What do I need to know to feel better?

Satisfy your emotional needs. This is the final requisite of *nonjudgment* that doesn't question what you need, nor mocks, belittles, or tries to talk you out of it. In his book *Hardwiring Happiness*, Dr. Rick Hanson writes that our emotional needs are loosely related to one of the three core needs that evolved through our collective journey: safety, satisfaction, and connection.

Depending on your answers in step 2, establish a sense of stability, reach out to others, or do one thing that makes you feel good. Or bring instances of feeing safe, capable, or loved to mind, and let the memories fill your empty cup until you're ready to step out as your best self.

Express the best version of yourself. Often, this happens naturally because we're hard-wired to grow into our greatest potential when we aren't hurting or feeling threatened. We'll do the work of creating this best version in the next chapter, but for now, here's a magical question that will help you express the best of yourself: **What's important now?**

In her latest book *Fierce Self-Compassion*, Dr. Kristen Neff writes that action that comes from a place of compassion tends to fall into one of three categories:[43]

1. **Protecting behaviors:** setting boundaries, saying no, speaking up for ourselves or others, asking for what we deserve, choosing to disengage from an argument/situation, leaving a space where we feel physically or psychologically unprotected.

2. **Motivating behaviors:** bringing about change in some aspect of our lives, taking steps toward our goals, setting new habits, reaching out to people who can help us, gaining skills or qualifications *that are needed* for our goals and not as a way of delaying action.

3. **Providing behaviors:** saying yes to our needs, cheering someone on, apologizing or making amends, bringing love to a person/situation we find triggering, working through anger mindfully, refraining from gossip and ill-will, appreciating the goodness in others.

I'd been practicing the RISE framework long enough to know what I needed to do as I sat in my room that October night feeling so small and insignificant inside. Within moments, I'd brought my loving presence to mind. I put both my hands on my heart with gentle pressure and softly repeated *I'm here, I'm here, I'm here* until my mental chatter was a faint sound somewhere in the distance.

Once calmer, I asked myself the one question that always seems to get the most honest reply: *What do you really need, my child?* From somewhere inside, I heard myself say, *I need to know it's going to be okay.* I hugged myself even tighter, my arms around me, and repeated, over and over, in a soft and reassuring voice, *It's going to be okay, my love. It's all going to be okay.*

The sobs came back, but this time, they were sobs of joy as my mind flooded with memories of the five of us, "the fab five" as we called ourselves, together through thick and thin. Could I really believe the story of rejection that my mind had been spinning all along? Hadn't we forgiven each other for far worse? And hadn't we grown even closer through it?

I got off the floor and walked out to the family room. I knew what I needed to do. My children looked up at me, not sure what to expect. I was together and coherent as I looked them in the eye and said, "I'm truly sorry about how I behaved. I know I shocked you and likely upset you as well because it really wasn't your fault.

The story I kept telling myself was that you didn't care about me, which was wrong. Will you forgive me?"

Of course, they did. We hugged and laughed and cried. Yes, they made fun of how I'd flipped my lid, but they also shared how much the weekend had meant to them and how touched they were by the efforts I'd put in. And they admitted, without me saying anything, that they should've checked in with me in the kitchen regardless.

It reminded me of the Persian poet Hafiz's quote:

> *"And still, after all this time,*
> *The sun never says to the earth,*
> *'You owe Me.'*
>
> *Look what happens with*
> *A love like that,*
> *It lights the Whole Sky."*[44]

Self-compassion is indeed a magical thing!

Chapter 5

Belonging with Others

Belonging to ourselves is where the work begins. We need to feel worthy within ourselves so we can be honest and vibrant in our relationships. We could have an amazing job, even one that feels purposeful and fulfilling. There's no doubt that we could have a great salary, the house of our dreams, and the ability to buy almost anything we want. But nothing can compensate for a poisonous relationship at work or at home.

We *need* each other to feel and to heal, to experience our joys and to grow into whole and integrated human beings because our mental frameworks of who we are are deeply intertwined with the people around us. Sadly though, insecure attachment does not set us up to do so. Instead of having a healthy balance of give and take, we experience an imbalance of power that makes it difficult to feel respected or to trust others.

Dr. Jennie Rosier, who studies the impact of childhood attachment styles on adult relationships, explains this imbalance in a 2x2 matrix with four quadrants. Few of us fall squarely in any one quadrant, nor are we the same with everyone. A relationship is, after all, about two or more people with their own baggage and thus its own beast. Even so, Dr. Rosier's research will help you see why you may be struggling in some of your relationships.

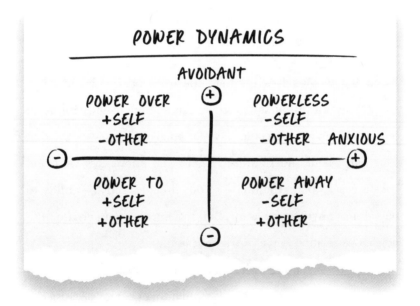

In fragile confidence, we tend to be mostly in the high avoidant/low anxious quadrant (stemming from avoidant attachment)

or the high anxious/low avoidant quadrant (based on anxious attachment). The former shows up as an overly favorable view of the self and a somewhat negative opinion of others. You see them as incapable, inferior, or hurdles to your success and happiness. These beliefs of superiority entitle you to have power *over* them.

In the latter, you have a high opinion of others and a low opinion of yourself and your abilities. This makes you clingy in your relationships and dependent on help, approval, or constant validation. As such, you give your power *away* to others.

Relational dynamics are also highly affected by the larger systems within which we operate. Consider the messages you received about relationships growing up. Were you raised to be more autonomous or more loyal to your family or friends? Was the importance of self-reliance emphasized in your life, or were you taught that relationships come first? We all receive such messages, sometimes overtly, and sometimes in the way we see the adults do things.

Most times, these messages are impacted by the cultures we grow up in; gender socialization begins in our homes. Maybe your brothers were encouraged to go out and explore the world, while you were raised to be likable and talented, so you find a good partner. Or maybe you saw a female cousin or aunt ostracized by the family because she decided to pursue her ambitions instead of settling down and starting a family.

We also experience power dynamics within the family structure. Most of us grew up at a time when there were very defined hierarchies, not only in the child–caregiver relationship, but often between siblings as well. My grandmother (Dadima) made sure I called my older brother "bhaijan," a title given to someone much older and highly revered. Bhaijan is barely one and half older than me!

These days, power dynamics within families are far more fluid. Every so often, I'm taken aback by what my children can say to me, usually in good humor, and think, *I could NEVER have said that to my mom!* However, power dynamics in workplaces are still hierarchical for the most part, especially in collectivist cultures where there are strict protocols to who can speak and when they can do so.

Most of these relational dynamics disadvantage women because of the millennia we have spent being silenced, sidelined, and subjugated to inferior treatment. No wonder, even the most opinionated or confident among us can crumble eventually in the lop-sided power equation of these larger systems.

Tara was in her early thirties and an associate at an investment bank. She had recently migrated to Canada without her family to make a life for herself. She was ambitious, vocal, and during our first session, I could see that she had a predominantly avoidant attachment style. Her professional growth was the only real focus of her life. She had never been in a serious romantic relationship, and later told me, "I find it hard to open up. I'm not even sure I want to."

She came to me because of an incident at work that had totally derailed her. She'd been just about three weeks into her current job when she'd learned about a job opening at another investment bank that ranked higher and paid somewhat better. She was eager to interview for them but naturally didn't want the seniors on her team to find out. So she shared her plans with her colleagues (the juniors), hoping they'd be impressed and trusting they'd cover up for her.

They didn't, and word got out. Tara crumbled. She was mad that some of them didn't safeguard her secret and terrified that she may lose her job. But she didn't have the courage to bring it up with them because she felt less powerful in the relationship. "I'm sure they thought of me as some naive and stupid immigrant." She hoped desperately that she would get the job she had interviewed for, so she didn't have to face them again. It also felt like a good comeback for the breach of trust.

When she didn't get the job, she became engulfed in shame and wanted to quit, even though she desperately needed the income. Our work was much deeper than the situation she found herself in. It was about building the solid ground of self-worth because indiscriminate sharing happens in any situation we enter from a place of inferiority. It is common in anxious attachment where we consider others to be more worthy or capable. We expose ourselves a little too soon to win their allegiance. Even though Tara had a predominantly avoidant attachment style, the larger relational dynamics had flipped power *over* to power *away*.

A ME IN A WE

Let's unpack what power means, because it's not what most of us assume it to be. We tend give it a "winner takes all" connotation, and for good reason. The people we see in power, in our leadership and sometimes in our homes, are the ones who get their way at the expense of others, blame and criticize those who speak up, and walk around with a sense of entitlement.

However, power is not a bad thing in and of itself. Esther Perel, the famed psychotherapist who explores the tension between intimacy and independence in relationships, states that power is neutral and inherent in every relationship. **What you do with the power is what matters.** A parent who gives their power to a child from a place of trust can help the child spread their wings and fly. Power away becomes power *to*. But when it happens from a place of inferiority or incompetence, it creates a power vacuum, and the child sometimes ends up being the parent.

Power away can also become power *over*. You've likely experienced it if there are people in your life who are unable or unwilling to manage their own lives. Their inability to regulate their emotions, manage their time, or take care of their work or relationships somehow places the onus on *you* to do so. You start running around making sure they're happy or on track. Sometimes we create such situations, and helicopter parenting is one such example. Children who do not get a chance to fight their own battles do not learn how to do so. Even when the parent is ready to hand over the reins, they feel trapped by the incompetence of their child.

Similarly, power over is a double-edged sword. It can be used to judge, demean, criticize, or hold others in contempt. This is often the power that comes from deep-seated feelings of unworthiness. Hurt people hurt people.

But power over can also be a beautiful thing when used generatively. We see it all the time in relationships bound by threads of security and worthiness, where one person uses their power to make life better for the other person. This again is power *to*.

When we see others as worthy, and value them for who they are, we're attuned to their needs and aspirations instead of judging them for the role they play in the relationship. Power can then flow freely from one person to the other because we're all playing roles within our relationships all the time.. In our home growing up, my father was the bread earner, and my mother was the homemaker. But my mother shared the power equally, because my father valued her for who she was, instead of measuring her worth through her competence or financial contribution.

Insecure attachment not only makes us judgmental, it also blinds to our judgments in areas of self-worth dependency. Research on the overconfidence bias shows that over 80 percent of people are pretty darn sure of themselves when there's a disagreement.[45] Religion and politics are more susceptible to rigid and extreme beliefs because they're mostly driven by subconscious feelings. We use facts and logic to simply corroborate what we feel at an implicit level. Not to change it.

We also live in a world where facts reign over feelings. There's been an almost inverse relationship between progress (as we've come to define it) and heartfelt connection, where we're able to see others in their full humanity. John Powell, internationally recognized expert in the areas of civil liberties, structural racialization, and democracy, talks about the systematic breaking of human bonds based on gender, race, religion, sexual orientation, political affiliation, age, color, size, disability, and a whole host of "isms." He calls it the process of "othering."[46]

Much of this is also impacted by the world order that has been around for centuries. In 2010, three psychologists introduced the acronym WEIRD to point out the over-representation of Western, Educated, Industrialized, Rich, and Democratic societies in our understanding of the world. This biased understanding influences the causes we pursue, the issues we pay attention to, the teachings we follow, and the values we uphold.

Most importantly, it impacts the ways in which we interact with those "not like us".

In his book *Ich und Du* (I and Thou), philosopher Martin Buber described three types of relational dynamics:[47]

1. An **I-Thou** relationship is one where you're able to see and respect your own humanity and your needs and aspirations alongside those of the other. It's how people with secure attachment relate to each other.

2. An **I-It** relationship is one where you take your own needs and pursuits seriously but play down or belittle those of the other. It also has an inverse, the **It-Thou** relationship where you undervalue, neglect, or sacrifice your own needs, emotions, passions, or aspirations for the other person.

3. An **It-It** relationship is one where both people are as indifferent or judgmental of their own needs and vision as they are of those of the other. This is the more clinical version of insecure attachment.

The magic of relationships lies in advocating for both I and Thou, where each person feels seen, where their emotional and soulful needs are recognized, and where there's a commitment to each other's growth and happiness. This is constant work—the central task of growing up according to developmental psychologist Gordon Neufeld.

If you're feeling stuck or unhappy in a relationship, it's likely because you've been denying your own needs or been blind to those of the other. This is true for all relationships because work and life are not that different after all. In her new podcast *How's Work?*, Esther Perel says that our relational dowry from the past is the unofficial résumé we bring to work. For years, I've worked with women who bring the same fears and frustrations to the boardroom as to the bedroom, to office meetings and to family picnics. Sure, they may show up differently because of the context or the person they're with. But they shape our expectations, boundaries, levels of trust, and degree of communication, collaboration, and accountability.

ADVOCATING FOR "I"

In a webinar sometime back, I asked the couple hundred or so attendees whether they'd heard this phrase growing up: "I didn't expect this from you." I kind of knew what to expect, but I was taken aback by how fast and furiously the chat moved. Decades hadn't blurred the memory nor the impact of those words. Women wrote about being told their tone was "too brash," their ambitions "too high," their asks "too selfish." One of them wrote about being told she was "too needy," and that created its own little #MeToo movement.

After the webinar, one woman reached out to me. She said she felt strangled in the almost nonexistent space between her work and family life. She was in a senior marketing role at a tech firm in Seattle, and her train ride home to her twin boys was a nonstop email and Slack session. By the time she arrived at her doorstep, she was spent. Her little ones, though, were bubbling with energy and ready for fun time with mom. It usually ended with more fatigue, resentment, and the occasional emotional meltdown.

I asked her if there was a way she could take a break between her work life and home life. She said she would love to stop for a bit at a café that was right outside her final subway stop on the way home. "I've always wanted to do that," she said, and I noticed an energy in her voice. Almost instantly, she followed it with: "But I can't; it's too much of an ask." Our personal temperament, early experiences and societal expectations have created a cauldron into which we routinely throw our needs and desires until there is no "me" left in the relationship.

To preserve a me, we need boundaries. They are a relational imperative. But before we go about telling people where their space ends and ours begins, we need to know how far we're going to allow other people into our lives, because there's no clear-cut formula. Boundaries are situational, depending on who we're with and what's at stake. They are also porous. We cannot draw walls around us because relationships are essential to our well-being and growth.

The only way you can know what feels safe and what doesn't is to listen to the messages coming from your body. Research on the polyvagal nerve shows that we have nerve sensors in the gut and around the heart that pick up cues in their own way. They tell us when to move in and when to move away. But you cannot be attuned to your body's signals if you're already afraid or stressed out. You'll see threat where it doesn't exist, and it'll become a self-fulfilling prophesy. Or you'll get overwhelmed by the threat that does exist, and this will impact your ability to do something about it.

In her hilarious talk "This Lousy World," Tibetan Buddhist teacher Pema Chödrön describes how our frustration at the world makes us want to lock everything and everyone out of our lives.[48] A far better strategy, she says, is to protect our inner space so we can engage with the world with our values. Because when you feel safe and calm deep inside, you're able to assess clearly what feels unsafe in the outside world and set your boundaries accordingly.

CREATING INNER SAFETY

Sometime back, a young woman reached out to me for coaching. She said she was a UX developer at a large tech company, and in the two years she'd been at the firm, she had started losing the confidence she once had in her abilities. "I love my work," she said. "And I think I'm good at it. But when I'm with the other developers in the room, I start feeling I'm not as smart as them. They're loud and like to talk about their code, and it kind of throws me off."

It turned out she was a highly sensitive person (HSP) who became quickly overstimulated by the noise around her. But it is not only HSPs who struggle with external input. Empaths and introverts also experience emotional overload, as do most women when we're around people because of the way we're wired. Our spatial awareness attunes us to subtle cues and expressions, which can overwhelm our physiology and launch a cascade of emotions, especially if the cues touch upon feelings of inadequacy or rejection.

It's why many women are fine expressing themselves in situations that relate to strategic planning or cognitive processing but they become frazzled when emotions enter the scene. "I can't have a conversation with my teenager without reacting like one," a client confided last week. Others talk about the tears and blanking out and panic attacks when asking for a raise or promotion or sharing something personal.

PRACTICE

If that's you, here's how you can create inner safety before you engage in courageous conversations: begin with the breath. When you slow the breath down and breathe from your belly, it sends your body the message that you're safe. Often, that's all you need to do. And sometimes, you'll also need to address your thoughts because thoughts, emotions and physiology are all tightly interconnected. In her work on courage and daring leadership, Brené Brown suggests asking ourselves: "What's the story I'm telling myself?" I love this question because inherent in it is the choice to believe your story or not to believe it. **It returns the power back to you.**

For the young woman who came to me, this meant honoring her need for quiet and carving out moments in her day for mindful breathing, or to work in a segregated office versus the shared workspace. It also meant catching her story of "I'm incompetent, I don't know what I'm doing here" when someone got excited because their code had passed, and challenging it with "I've been hired for my expertise, I belong here."

The reality is that more often than not, it's not a situation but the stories you tell yourself about it that stop you from doing the things you want to do. When you learn to catch your stories, you realize how much rubbish the mind can spew. Even if there's some truth to it, it's usually hidden beneath a whole lot of exaggerations.

Here are some questions from cognitive behavioral therapy that will help you challenge your stories:

Is this story true? What's the evidence for it? What's the evidence against it? What is the full story? Do I need to do something about it, or can I safely let it go?

Is this story helpful? Is it helping me show up as who I want to be in this situation? Who do I want to be in this situation? What's a story that will help me do so?

You can use these questions for any situation where you doubt yourself or are playing small. Listen to the story you're telling yourself. What are you saying about your abilities or what people think of you? The purpose is not to seek out lies or fabricate a truth that doesn't exist. It's to see the **full** story, so you can decide what to do about the situation.

Say your boss didn't acknowledge you at the meeting this morning. Before you go down the rabbit hole of anger or rumination, catch the story you're telling yourself. Do you spot judgment (*She's known to have favorites*), self-doubt (*I think I'm not right for this team*) or shame (*No one likes me, I'm just odd*)? If so, challenge these stories so you arrive at the truth which is always more nuanced.

Maybe she didn't sleep well last night. Maybe she's preoccupied about an upcoming client meeting. Or maybe yes, there *is* some tension in the relationship, and you need to clear it up with her.

Because not all issues are to be dropped and not all threats to be taken lightly. Take microaggressions for example, a common phenomenon for women in the workplace. Microaggressions are subtle and not-so-subtle words and expressions meant to belittle, sideline, or silence women and other marginalized groups. Cynthia Barnes, founder and CEO of the National Association of Women Sales Professionals, breaks down these microaggressions into three categories:

1. **Micro assaults:** name calling, purposeful discriminatory actions, likely to be conscious and deliberate.
2. **Micro insults:** subtle snubs based on cultural stereotypes, sometimes innocent and frequently unknown to the person.
3. **Micro invalidations:** disconfirming messages that exclude, negate, or dismiss the feelings, opinions, or experiences of the other. *This is often the most damaging, the most common, and the most unacknowledged.*

To speak up against microaggressions, you need to first calm your inner space. Only then can you speak with power, instead of spewing it all out or staying silent when you need to raise your voice.

SPEAKING UP

We've already touched on the double bind of likability and competence that holds many women back from speaking up, or for being heard and respected for doing so. Deep-seated cultural biases do not make it easy for high potential, ambitious, and purpose-driven women to make an impact.

And yet the biases, and their resulting inequitable systems of power, will not change on their own. To bring about much-needed systemic change, women need a seat at the highest tables. And to get there, they have to speak up and advocate for themselves.

This can feel like a catch-22 situation. But I believe there is an effective way to maneuver through it, based on the Thomas Kilmann conflict model.[49] The model consists of two dimensions: assertiveness and cooperativeness. It states that when we are only assertive, we come across at competitive, and we know that this works against women. It also states that when we're only cooperative, we end up accommodating others at our own expense. Hence the double bind.

Most of our strategies thus far have been about doing a little of both to find the right balance. But this, according to the model, leads to a compromise on what's important. **The secret of effective collaboration, it appears, lies in dialing up both assertiveness and cooperativeness to their max.**

This goes against the advice many women receive when they rise in seniority. More than once, clients have told me that the training they receive when they move into managerial positions focuses solely on assertiveness. Some have even been told to dial down their empathy. No wonder they come up against resistance.

PRACTICE

The framework below will help you optimize both dimensions so you arrive at a win-win outcome. You can adapt it to almost any conversation, whether it is setting a boundary, asking for a raise, or having a difficult conversation someone in your life.

1. **What** do I need?

The first step is to get clear on what you need. What is making you unhappy or frustrated? What would you like instead? Many of us can struggle with this question for a variety of reasons. For starters, there's neurology; maybe you're the kind of person who is basically okay with anything. You're happy to go along with other people's choice of restaurant or movies without feeling you lost out in any way. Then there's the impact of early experiences where insecure attachment can make us unattuned to our needs. There's also gender socialization—women need to be agreeable and compliant, which can also disconnect us from what we want. And finally, the impact of a hurried world where few of us have time for introspection.

Being clear about your need makes it possible to be clear in your ask. Be careful not to start negotiating yourself down at this stage or convincing yourself asking. Many of us tend to do so, because of the biological fear of rejection, combined with the personal, anecdotal, and generational baggage of having spoken up and been ignored. Or faced adverse consequences for it.

If you find yourself doing so, talk to a trusted friend who understands your situation but is emotionally disconnected with it. They can offer you the perspective and courage you need, and also hold you accountable to do what you need to do.

2. **Why** is it important?

A why that's based in our values is powerful because values are part of who we are, how we define ourselves, and what's important to us. They need no justifications, no convincing, no arguments with our fears.

For women in particular, a why that is prosocial and benefits others makes us more courageous because relationships are a source of women's confidence. I remember a client who shared that the only time that she ever had the courage to speak up was when she needed to protect her little brother from her mother's drunken outbursts.

Regardless of whether you want to speak up against a microaggression, negotiate a raise, or ask for more time or space, think of why it's important for those you love or lead. Even an apparently "selfish" ask (more time to yourself) can benefit others—maybe it helps you be less on edge with your partner, more present with your children, or more focused in your work. Jennifer Crocker's research shows that moving from "ego to eco" (from yourself to the people around you) builds your confidence and your sense of self-worth.[50]

3. **Who** will I ask?

The next step is to be strategic in who you reach out to. Sometimes it's pretty evident, but sometimes you need to think of the people who can best support you in getting your needs met. For example, if you'd like an earlier bedtime, you need to let the family know so everyone's on board with an earlier dinner. Similarly, if you're experiencing gender bias at work, the best person to reach out to may be a male boss who is a proponent of equal treatment and women's advancement.

Deciding who to ask also requires understanding the person you are going to approach. How do they like to be approached? When is usually a good time to talk to them? What's important to them, and how does your ask fit into their values, worldview, or goals? This also helps with the next step of how to ask.

4. **How** will I ask?

The how has two important components. The first is what you say and how you make your ask appealing to the other person's heart and mind. Although this can vary depending on the situation, I've found that certain generalizations can apply. If your ask is an emotional one (more care, more understanding, etc.), let them know how having it, or not having it, makes you feel. Be careful not to blame—it will instantly make them defensive.

If it is about a job, raise, or promotion, make sure you let them know what's in it for them. Understand what they want so you can show them why you're the right person for it. And if you're trying to persuade the other person to take action on what's important to you, make them think it was their idea. It's a brilliant strategy that author Daniel Pink outlines in his book *To Sell Is Human*.[51]

Another equally important part of the verbal component is to be specific in your ask. It's all too common to float over the details or speak in generalizations and end up frustrated when we don't get exactly what we want. In work situations, it allows you to delegate better, which is a key skill of effective management. Be specific about timelines, what the end product looks like, even what you do not want to see.

The second component is about *the way* you ask: your speech patterns, body language, eye contact, and other subtle ways you can make or break your message. In her book *Playing Big*, women's leadership expert Tara Mohr talks about common and unhelpful speech patterns that undermine a woman's message:[52]

Hedges: *Just, actually, kind of.*

Apologies: *Sorry, but, Just a little, A little bit.*

Qualifying phrases: *I'm no expert, but, I could be wrong, but, Does that make sense?*

Undermining structures: Uptalk and singsongy tone, speaking too fast, substituting a question for a statement.

For many of us, these speech patterns become a "safety blanket" that help us have the more courageous conversations. But the reality is that we disrespect our message when we try to tone it down. It loses its power, and as in Thomas Killman's model, we end up compromising or accommodating.

If that's true for you, practice speaking without your safety blanket in nonthreatening situations—in front of a mirror, with a close friend or partner, or with a colleague or boss who knows you are working on being more assertive.

Practice gives you feedback, makes the behavior more natural, and gives you the courage to do so in more difficult situations. And–*this is important*–complement your more assertive style with a show of cooperation. Smile more. Listen better. Project empathy and understanding. Bingo!

5. **When** will I remind them?

Not all our asks will be accepted, and that's okay. The key is to leave the door open to revisit the ask. Executive leadership coach Marshall Goldsmith engages his clients in a feed *forward* process, where the other person becomes a partner in getting you what you want. Say your ask was a promotion, and it wasn't accepted. Ask your boss what she would like to see differently to make it happen. Update her regularly in your efforts. And ask again when you're ready.

Being proactive about reminding is also something that invariably comes up in the work around boundaries. Most people assume that once they've done the courageous work of asking, others will scurry around making sure we get what we want. It doesn't work that way. People will generally revert to the way things were because they genuinely forget. The brain works to conserve energy, and remembering new habits is hard work. Besides, people are processing a lot these days; remembering what others want or would want isn't easy.

I'm reminded of this every time I hope my kids did the vacuuming without me having to ask. Like most people, they wait until they're reminded, and it drives me up the wall. "If you cared about me, you'd do it," I hear myself saying. It's a silly argument, and it hasn't worked to this day.

If we want others to honor our asks, respect our boundaries, or give us the space we need to grow within the relationship, we need to take responsibility for helping it happen. This means two things in particular:

1. Gently point out every time they forget. Do not shame or blame. Be generous in your assumptions. Don't take things personally. They likely simply forgot.
2. Show your appreciation when they remember. Or reward them in some other way. It creates a dopamine surge in the brain that makes the behavior easy to repeat.

MOVING PAST RESENTMENT

A section on advocating for ourselves would be incomplete without addressing resentment, because resentment is often the by-product of not getting our needs met in a relationship. And while resentment may involve anger and hurt, it's the distinct feeling that others got the tall end of the bargain and we couldn't do anything about it.

Maybe they lied, maybe they cheated, or maybe they got certain advantages that we didn't and it harmed us in some way. In a world where women, and especially minority women or those from other marginalized groups, are unfairly disadvantaged at work, in society, or even in their homes, resentment isn't only common, it's also healthy. If we didn't feel resentful, we would accept our lot and stay trapped at the bottom of a patriarchal hierarchy.

What's unhealthy about it is that it keeps us stuck in the past and feeds feelings of victimization, helplessness, and negativity that keep us from speaking up for what's right. Sometimes, the people we feel resentful toward may not even be aware of how they've harmed us. Or if they are, they may not care or feel they've done what needs to be done, even though it's barely scratched the surface of the injustice.

To live our lives fully, even if it means accepting certain things we can't change or staying silent because its unsafe or not possible to speak up, we need to work through the resentment. It's bad enough to have been wronged. It's really not necessary to stay preoccupied with the pain and suffering it caused us. We needlessly give our power *away* to people who may or may not want to help us or who may no longer be around to do so.

I remember, a long time ago, being consumed by the hurt caused by a family member who had recently passed away. I couldn't sleep, I started having nightmares, and I felt I had no energy for my four little kids, who deserved a happy and energetic parent to attend to their needs.

One day, I shared my feelings of resentment with a friend during our walk back from dropping the kids off to school. She listened patiently—and I say patiently because I kept going round and round in circles with my endless list of grievances. Finally, she said, "Why do you give your power away to someone who is dead?"

I needed to hear that. I came home and asked myself how I wanted to feel in my life. Who did I want to be as a person? Did I like the bitter, resentful, snappy person I was becoming? Or did I want to live life with an open heart and with the grace of someone who can take life's knocks and bruises without becoming diminished by them?

That night, I did a little "closure" thing to help put the past behind me. I wrote down everything I felt hurt about in a diary. In fact, I wrote for five nights straight, while tears rolled down my cheeks for the innocent me who had tried hard in the relationship but not felt seen for who she was. I later learned about the therapeutic effects of writing; social psychologist James Pennebaker's research shows that putting emotional experiences into words has a cathartic effect and can help heal the pain of past experiences.[53]

On the sixth day, I tore out the pages from the diary and took them out in my garden. Way at the back, I dug a deep hole. Then page by page, I tore them up into tiny pieces and buried them deep inside. I sat there for a while, feeling a lot lighter. Finally, I got back up, and before turning away, I promised myself to not let the past haunt my present again.

For years after, the resentment lived in a small and distant corner of my life. It showed up now and again but lacked the sharp edges that had cut right through my heart. Now, it's been replaced by a kind of warmth, a forgiveness for the person they were because of the many external forces that made them that way. And it's the forgiveness that has brought me a lasting sense of peace.

We often confuse forgiving with forgetting even though they are not the same thing. Forgiving is about advocating for ourselves. It's about taking a stand for our own emotional well-being. It's about refusing to let ourselves be burned by the coals that others have thrown at us. Forgetting is about making ourselves vulnerable to more coals, if the person is still capable of throwing them. Until you've built back the lost trust in a relationship, it's wise to remember without becoming consumed by the hurt. Working through resentments allows you to do so.

PRACTICE

If you're feeling resentful toward somebody in your life, begin by directing love and compassion toward yourself. You're hurting and you need yourself by your side. As we saw in the previous chapter, self-compassion expands our perspective and helps us lead with our values. Then ask yourself these questions:

What was the injustice?

How bad was the injury?

How does the behavior make sense given their situation or the societal context?

What may I have done if I were in their shoes/had their level of awareness?

How did I contribute to the hurt? (not speaking up for myself, turning away, gossiping, etc.)

What part did I play in the situation? **It's empowering to own your part, because then you can do something to make things better.**

Once you're ready, and it may take time, ask yourself what you will do to move forward as your biggest self. Maybe you'll say a silent prayer that wishes them well in order to let go of the hurt. Maybe you'll bring it up with them, be open and vulnerable in your sharing, and stay curious to what comes up. Maybe you'll set boundaries and either let them know about them ("I'm asking for..." or "I want you to...") or simply know them yourself ("I'll make sure I don't..."). Your response will be based on the situation and how *you* want to show up in the world.

ADVOCATING FOR "THOU"

Advocating for others, whether it is speaking up for them or leaning into a difficult moment or conversation, happens in the safe container of trust. And research shows that trust, thankfully, doesn't require gigantic feats of altruism. It is built one small step at a time.

When somebody shares something with you, be it a grudge, an apology, a request, a story, a joke, or a moment of tenderness, humiliation, or shame, they've instantly made themselves vulnerable to your emotions, judgments, and reactions. They've given their power *to* you and are hoping you can make them feel safe in their sharing. It feels vulnerable because they've exposed their neediness and are at the mercy of your response.

When you're attuned with their emotions and respond in a way that makes them feel safe, it adds a little marble to what Brené Brown calls the marble jar of trust. They can then be more emotionally vulnerable in their sharing, and your empathic response further fills their jar. The research shows that trust and emotional vulnerability work in feedback loops. I like to think of them like walking—each step happens because of the other and fails to happen without the other. We can't get very far when one foot is tied to a pole.

One person's emotional vulnerability also gives the other person the courage and permission to be vulnerable. And when their vulnerability is met with the same attuned and helpful response—because we're wired for reciprocity—it creates these bigger feedback loops of a trusting *relationship* that's based on mutual care, respect, and support.

Empathy thus is the milieu in which it all happens. And empathy needs to be cultivated, because as we saw earlier, we're often judgmental, and sometimes without even knowing it.

BUILDING EMPATHY

Most of us engage in what sociologist Martha Beck calls "ear listening." Ear listening is about scanning for information that confirms what we already believe or that's important for our survival: "I knew he'd say that. Why does he always have to show he's right?" Or, "She didn't show much support for my idea. I guess it was dumb. I should never have suggested it." Fragile confidence or not, it's how many of us listen because we've evolved for survival.

To build trusting relationships that help us *thrive*, we need to move into the deeper layers of listening that Dr. Beck calls "body" and "heart listening." Body listening is reading other people's bodily cues (are they looking away, breathing heavily, restless or anxious?) and making sure our bodily cues are making them feel safe.

Where and how we look is extremely important because human beings are the only mammals who have such prominent sclera—the whites of eyes. They helped our ancestors warn each other about danger by simply looking in a certain direction without having to make sounds, which may have made the situation worse. Looking at your digital device while they're talking doesn't help. Nor does looking at them in a judgmental or threatening way.

I had a client sent to me by the HR department because some of the company's clients had complained about her unfriendly style of communication. I asked for a video recording of a client meeting and noticed that she frowned every time their client spoke.

At our coaching session, we watched the video together and I shared my observation. She was completely taken aback and remarked: "I was paying close attention, that was all!" The relationship changed dramatically for the better once she worked on her facial expression.

Heart listening goes even deeper and brings empathy into the mix. Many people fear that empathy means agreement or compromising and giving up what they believe is right. It's not. It's bigger than that. It's about saying *I feel with you* regardless of whether I understand your situation or agree with your approach.

In her autobiography *The Story of My Life*, the deaf, dumb, and blind political activist and disability rights advocate Helen Keller describes the feeling of being seen when her teacher Anne Sullivan touched her.[54] As human beings, we can feel seen even if the other person doesn't say a word. That is the true essence of empathy, beautifully encapsulated in the South African term *sawobona*, that's generally used as a greeting. It translates to: "Until I'm seen, I'm not here."

Empathy is the epitome of power to for many reasons. One, when we're seen, we become unhooked from whatever emotion is keeping us stuck and can engage our higher order thinking capacities. Secondly, when the other person is empathic to our needs, they can help us in a way that works for us. Funnily enough, this doesn't happen often. How many times have you been at the receiving end of someone's "help" that wasn't helping you at all? They were trying to be of service by doing what works for them.

There is one more reason empathy is empowering for the receiver. When we engage our hearts, we can give feedback that challenges the other person to rise to their potential because we value their strengths, qualities, vision, and dreams. Without empathy, we tend to be judgmental or take things personally when people underperform or act out their fears or biases.

PRACTICE

Here are a few ways of building empathy. See which one(s) feels right for you in the situation you find yourself in:

Look at Them

One of the easiest (and most overlooked) ways of building empathy is by looking at the person talking to you. People's facial expressions and body language help us understand their pain, joy, frustrations, and aspirations because most communication is non-verbal.

Play Detective

When someone talks to you, try to identify the need beneath the words. This is important because sometimes what people need is not conveyed in their words or actions. For example, moping, being aggressive or withdrawing can all be calls for more love and attention. Playing detective helps because curiosity and judgment cannot co-exist.

Invite Love In

This is a lovely practice I learned early on in mindfulness training. It's about purposefully engaging a prosocial virtue because these virtues are inherent in all of us. You can even say something like "Love, will you please enter the room?" If you find that corny, think of all the not so helpful things you say to yourself, and your mind's willingness to believe them.

Be Their Advocate

This practice engages cognitive empathy (versus emotional empathy), also called perspective-taking. Pretend you're the other person's lawyer, in charge of defending their case. What will you say in their favor? How will you justify their behaviors? What made them do what they did?

Notice the Good

This practice works particularly well if someone triggers you, because when we're triggered, we become consumed by the things we don't like about the other person. Noticing the good in them, even if the good isn't toward you, allows you to see the *whole* person. This perspective takes the edge off the "bad" and makes you less judgmental.

Loving Kindness Meditation

There's mounds of research to show the benefits of Loving Kindness Meditation in opening our hearts and making them more receptive. It is especially helpful if your relationship is mired in hurt and grievances. When you soften your heart, you can hold space for the other person's faults and weaknesses. You can judge their actions, but not their worth.

SUPPORTING OTHERS

At a Women's Day event a couple of years ago, I was invited to give a talk at the Center for Women's Leadership, University of

Arizona Global Campus. The topic was women's allyship, what it is, what it's not, and how we can help each other play bigger in the workplace. I gave my twenty-minute spiel, and then we opened up for Q and A. I was expecting questions around what I'd shared, maybe some deeper insights into the research around allyship, especially in the light of supporting women across differences in identity. Little did I know what I was in for.

One after the other, women spoke about female bosses who were mean and unsupportive, about being backstabbed by other women in their workplaces, about cattiness and "frenemies"— women who pretended to be allies but were anything but. It was like the entire auditorium was saying, "All that's fine and dandy. But that's not our lived experience."

Since then, I've spoken to hundreds of women about how supported they've felt by female colleagues and bosses. I've read countless studies and conducted my own surveys. And I've come to the view that for women in particular, **lifting and rising need to happen hand in hand**. We're all sitting atop millennia of hurt and denial around expressions of female autonomy. In our personal and collective lives, we've had to tamp down our needs, desires, dreams, and aspirations in the name of tradition, culture, religion, and values. And these tamped down, suffocated parts of ourselves will not, cannot, allow in others what wasn't allowed to us or what we don't allow in ourselves.

This is not just in our work around supporting other women. I've seen it among friends, in families, and in intimate relationships. Say a partner wants to lose weight, reduce their alcohol intake, or expand their social group. Unless the other is happy with that aspect of their own life or isn't facing obstacles, internal or external, to work on it, they'll become an impediment to their partner's goals.

Giving others permission to grow begins with giving ourselves permission to do the same. If you find yourself feeling jealous or angry at someone else's success, backbiting, engaging in gossip, sharing their secrets, labeling them as brash or selfish or power hungry, being restrained in your expressions of joy at their success, or being outright negative about it, it's time to step back and check in with yourself:

What in me am I denying?
What needs to feel seen?
What needs expression?
How will I do so?

Sometimes, there's grief around unseen or unexpressed parts of ourselves. You may recall the younger you who had to work so hard for things that others get far more easily. One of my clients felt resentful of the juniors on her team who could work flex hours when they wanted. She recalled her own struggles with taking care of three little ones while working full time and the guilt of leaving them with a neighbor when they weren't well enough to go to day care. If similar emotions come up for you, bring your inner compassion to mind, and work through your feelings of grief.

Resistance can also happen in the I-it relationship that emerges in avoidant attachment. You believe that the other growth hampers yours, or that you are the only one in the relationship who is entitled to happiness or success. This resistance, as mentioned back in chapter 1, is harder to work with because avoidant attachment leaves little room for doubt. You actually believe you're better, more capable, or more deserving—beliefs you formed a long time ago to mask the pain of not mattering to those who mattered the most to you.

The other side of the same coin is the woman who isn't supportive of your growth or well-being. What in her needs celebrating? What in her life may she be tamping down? Or had to tamp down to get to where she is? Maybe she had to overcome a lot more organizational barriers to her advancement. Maybe she didn't have the help or resources that you do. Or maybe she carries the feelings of entitlement that emerge from unprocessed hurt. It doesn't justify her actions, but they make more sense. And sense making unhooks us from the other person's resistance and frees us to do the things that advance our growth. You may even be able to relate to her with compassion, which can free her of the hurt she's likely been lugging around for decades.

While this first aspect of women not supporting each other is very real, there's a second aspect that's more of a perception based on similar cultural beliefs and expectations. Many of us will consider negative feedback from a male boss to be "advice" and that from a female boss to be "criticism." We'll expect the women to be warm and agreeable in their mannerisms and feel attacked when they challenge us. We'll want them to be sensitive and understanding of our mistakes or challenges, because after all, they're part of our "tribe." The least breach of this unspoken contract and our hunter–gatherer brain feels stabbed by one of its own kind. Faulty perceptions are a breeding ground for mistrust.

These perceptions are instinctive because their underlying beliefs are outside our conscious awareness. Even after years of research and practice, my very first reaction to a woman being direct, ambitious, or unemotional is often one of dislike. Sometimes, I hear myself thinking *I don't think I can trust her* or *I'm sure her kids are suffering as a result.* If you have similar reactions, or if you cringe at the thought of being assertive or forceful in the way you challenge your kids or your team, take a deep breath and smile. It's okay. Your feelings exist for a reason. And your thoughts are servicing them.

Your work is to recognize the thoughts, and instead of denying or defending them, to bring compassion and curiosity around them so you can show up as the person you want to be.

This is the important work we need to do around supporting women across differences in identity as well. Before we can lift other women, we have to become aware of our beliefs around sexual orientation, class, race, age, and other forms of bias that are interwoven with patriarchy. We have to recognize our instinctual reactions and be honest in acknowledging them, even if it's just to ourselves. Only then can we distance ourselves from generational beliefs and biases and be the ushers of a new world of mutual belonging.

LIFTING OTHERS

Dr. Meg Warren's award-winning research on allyship at Western Washington University highlights the gap in many workplace diversity, equity, and inclusion (DEI) policies; marginalized groups do not simply want privileged groups to protect them from the negative.[55] In fact, an overemphasis on protection can actually derail DEI efforts. They want, more than anything, to be seen and appreciated for the value they bring. And that's where most of our efforts fall short.

It's not enough to speak up for the woman who was spoken over. It's not enough to make sure your transgender colleague is invited to the team meeting or a client dinner. Because being included is different from belonging. Inclusion says you're welcome as long as you adhere to the standards that have already been created. Belonging says *I see you, I celebrate you, and I value what you bring to the table. Let's then create something beautiful together.*

To truly lift others, we first need to get to know them. What are their strengths and qualities, and what can we do to bring those to light? What are their aspirations and the legacy they want to leave behind? And what will we do to help them grow into the biggest version of who they can be? **Our job is to have the same fire in the belly for their dreams as they do.**

PRACTICE

Whether in parenting, in DEI work, or in any relationship you wish to build and nurture, you have to become genuinely curious about others and committed to bringing out the magic in them. Here are some conversations starters:

What have been some of the best moments of your life?

What are some of the qualities or strengths you would like to use more of?

What are your goals or aspirations? Why are these goals and aspirations important to you?

Who do you want to be? What kind of life do you want to live? What kind of impact do you want to have?

What are some of the challenges you're facing? What would need to change for you to show up more fully? Where can I help you?

Dr. Shelly Gable's work on active constructive responding provides another wonderful pathway to celebrate others. She and her colleagues at the University of California, Santa Barbara, have found that the best way to respond to someone's good news is by expressing our joy while also helping them take ownership of the success.[56] It's not just a "Yay, so happy for you!" It's also:

"Tell me more! What made you decide to go after that project?"

"I want to hear all about it! How did she come around, and how did you convince her?"

"Did you really? Oh my God, this shows such (an admirable quality)."

"What are some of the next steps for you? How are you going to build on this amazing news?"

Conversations such as these are extremely powerful for women in particular, because we need to be reminded of our strengths, qualities, and courage. They're also beautiful because seeing the magic in others helps us see the magic in ourselves. As

French philosopher Voltaire said, "Appreciation is a wonderful thing: it makes what is excellent in others belong to us as well."

MAKING REPAIRS

Just as a section on boundaries was incomplete with addressing resentment, a section on trust calls for addressing trust *repair*. Because making mistakes in our relationships is one of the few guarantees in life. We are, after all, two or more individuals relating to each other with our fears, faults, desires, preferences, stresses, and life constraints. Even if we do nothing wrong, the other can feel attacked or ignored because of their own perceptions and expectations. And that can impact our reactions, launching a downward spiral of broken trust.

The good news is that trust is reparable; making mistakes doesn't harm our relationships as long as we apologize *sincerely* right after. When we express our remorse and commitment to not repeating the mistake, we often end up adding more marbles to the trust jar than we took out.

Sadly though, most apologies don't do a good job at repair because they lack one or more of the components of a sincere apology. Here are three of the more common faulty ones:

Non-apology #1: The Disgrace

It's when we become so engulfed in shame by what we said

or did that we need to be rescued by the other person. We need *them* to make *us* feel better, which is not only difficult (try dragging someone out of self-pity mode), but also unfair, especially if the other person is still reeling from the hurt we caused them.

Non-apology #2: The Insistence

These are the appeasing and sympathy seeking reactions that beg for instant forgiveness. Unfortunately, that's not how it works; the other person has to be ready to move on. This is true even when you offer a sincere apology. You cannot force forgiveness, and sometimes your most heartfelt apology may need to sit on the ledge until the receiver is ready to accept it.

Non-apology #3: The Dismissal

It's when an apology, if offered, sounds more like *I'm sorry but you're just being too sensitive.* It's about shoving the blame onto the other person instead of taking responsibility for our part. Sometimes, there's also an element of educating them: *People say and do things like this all the time, you'd better grow a thicker skin if you want to survive in the world.*

What underpins these three non-apologies is the expectation that the other person does something—rescue us, forgive us, or fix themselves. If they don't, we may become offended, even aggressive, because we made ourselves vulnerable with the apology, and it wasn't met with empathy. We start throwing out marbles from *our* trust jar when our job is to add marbles to *theirs*. Here's how to do so.

PRACTICE

A sincere apology is made up of three essential steps.

Step 1: **Awareness**

Recognize your part without the moral blows of shame or blame. You'll need to invite your inner compassion to help you put things into perspective. She'll also help you with painful feelings because you do need to feel remorse in order to be sincere in your apology. Focus on the other person's feelings, whether justified in your mind or not.

Step 2: **Acknowledgment**

From this place of empathy and compassion, convey your remorse to the other person without justifications, partial blame, or sympathy seeking. Let them know that you recognize their hurt, but don't pretend to know how they feel. Because you don't. Every one suffers in their own way; your job is to make them feel seen. They'll likely be receptive to what you're going to say.

Step 3: **Amends**

The final step is to let them know what you're going to do to make sure the mistake isn't repeated. Be open to their feedback. Ask them whether they want something else from you. Don't fall into the temptation of telling them what you want *them* to do, unless they go there themselves. This is about taking responsibility to make things better.

Sometimes, though, we become aware of our mistakes when it's not possible or not advisable to apologize for them. The person who was hurt by your actions may be dead or unwilling to engage with you. Or they may be unaware of your role, and letting them know may cause more pain. When acknowledgment is not possible or wise, you still need to take action on the awareness. Else you will end up with regrets.

A while back, a friend sobbed during a visit as she shared the guilt she was carrying over the way she'd treated her mother-in-law in her final years of life. She'd never visited her in her nursing home even though she knew she was miserable there. And she minimized her husband's visits as well by telling him she'd already been that week, or setting up outings with friends or the kids so he didn't have time to go. *"What do I do about the guilt? It's killing me. I imagine her watching me from above and I can't look at myself. Its karma, I wish I had been a better person."*

I could feel her agony and knew that she'd stay trapped in the past unless she found a way to ease her suffering. I explained to her that sometimes the "acknowledgment" in an apology is silent. We ask for forgiveness in our hearts. And we trust that the energy will travel from one broken heart to the other and bring healing to both.

My friend began a daily practice of Loving Kindness Meditation because it extends love to self and others. She also began volunteering twice a week at the nursing home where her mother-in-law had eventually passed away. It was her "amend" and slowly but surely, she found healing.

THE INNER GUIDE

The presence that helps build healthy relationships of mutual support is an extension of the inner compassion, as are the other two presences as well. Unconditional love and understanding toward ourselves are irreducible and nonnegotiable qualities that underpin our ability to be the highest version of who we are.

I call this presence the inner guide because relationships are messy and complex, and sometimes we need someone to guide us past our immediate impulses and personal desires. She's the older, wiser version of us who is separated from the messiness of the present moment in both time and knowing. If the inner compassion is the microscope that helps us zoom in to what's important in this moment, the inner guide is the telescope who helps us zoom *out* to the bigger picture of our lives. She doesn't let ego get in the way of the universal hunger to love and to be loved.

Before you can access the wisdom of your inner guide, you'll need to create her. It's not something we're naturally wired to do. The human brain sees the future self as a separate self. We may know our goals, our dream job, or where we'd like to live or who we'd like to marry. But that knowledge isn't the same as knowing the person we'd like to be. That comes from stepping into our future lives and imagining who and how we are in it.

There's a fun way of doing so that I learned in my coach training many years ago. It's an imaginary exercise where you visit the older version of you, at least a decade or so in the future, so you're not influenced by the stresses and pursuits of your present life.

Some of these questions can help you imagine the person you'll meet:

How does it feel being in her presence?

How does she start her morning?

Who does she spend her time with?

What are her favorite conversations?

What ideals does she live by?

What are some of the lessons she's learned in life? How have they changed her for the better?

What is most powerful about her?

Where does she live?

How does she spend her day?

What does she love to wear?

Where does she spend her time? Does she have a favorite room in the house?

Creating this image isn't only helpful for solving a relational dilemma; it can also guide you in how you want to live. *What should I eat? What should I buy for my living room? What should I give Aunt Fanny for her birthday?*

ACCESSING THE INNER GUIDE

When you want a question answered, take some time to center yourself first. You cannot access your inner wisdom if you're frazzled, frustrated, or freaking out. Once you feel more grounded, take the journey to your inner guide. You can do so in any way you like—a stroll through the fields, a drive on a scenic highway, or, who knows, being airlifted to her home?

Now imagine yourself in her presence. Make it feel as real as possible—what's she wearing, where are you sitting, what has she offered you to eat or drink? When you're ready, here are three questions you will ask her. You can ask more for sure, but these three are important:

1. What can you tell me about [the dilemma you're facing]?
2. Is there anything else about this situation I need to know?
3. What is the one thing I need to remember as I work through it?

The answer may come in images or a feeling and not in words. Listen and accept whatever comes up, even if it feels weird or doesn't make sense to you. Sometimes it may not come at all for a while. That's okay too; trust that it will, as long as you don't try and rush it. Your protector parts will want to do that because they demand uncertainty: *I just need to know!* Recognize their voice and gently distance yourself from it.

Once you've had the conversation, you can thank your inner guide and then leave. Remember, you can go back to her anytime and for all kinds of challenges and dilemmas.

1. What career should I go into?
2. Is this risk worth taking?
3. Which strategy would be best for me?
4. Should I step back or step up?

We tend to go to other people for these kinds of questions. Sometimes this isn't helpful, because their answers may reflect their fears or biases. And sometimes it is, because others can help us expand our perspective. But eventually, the answer has to come from within us. We already have the wisdom, clarity, beauty, and courage we seek. It simply gets blocked or tamped down by all the external messages we receive endlessly.

In their book *Noise*, psychologist and economist Daniel Kahneman and coauthors claim that our head is not the right place for important decision-making.[57] Through scientific research and examples, they show that human judgment is flawed because our heads are bombarded by noise from the outside world, and from our own voices of fear. The best decision-making happens when we begin with our heads (making a list of the pros and cons between two or more choices, asking others for suggestions and advice, etc.), and then sit back, turn our minds off, and let intuition guide us. This is the role of the inner guide, because she's perhaps the only person who knows what we most long for.

WHO DO I WANT TO BE?

When I was a child, my father would tell me a story about my grandfather that took me decades to fully appreciate. A gentleman visited my grandfather, and in the hopes of winning his favor, this gentleman confided a piece of gossip that a common acquaintance had said about my grandfather.

Instead of engaging with the topic, or digging for more

information, my grandfather said politely, "You must be mistaken, my friend. [The common acquaintance] is a dear friend and would never say something like that about me."

It turned out the common acquaintance wasn't someone my grandfather knew that well. He had no way of knowing whether he would say such a thing or not. But his sense of self-worth was so solid that it didn't matter. He wasn't interested in walking through life looking for signs he wasn't loved or collecting proof that the world had let him down in some way. His trust in human goodness was far too deep for that.

We're wired for trust building. We come into the world ready to believe in the strength of our relationships. Even the game of peekaboo—a perennial favorite with all kids across the world—is about trusting that when we look again, the person will still be there. Those shrieks of joy, those squeals of gratification, are expressions of trust that say *I knew you'd be there for me!*

When trust building doesn't happen as nature intended, we need to notice and intentionally take in moments when someone listens compassionately, takes an interest in our lives, speaks up for us, praises something they like about us, doesn't complain about something they don't like in us, or maybe even says they're okay with it.

The more we do, the more we're able to give with an open

heart. To listen to the other person without being triggered by their words or behaviors. To give them importance when they speak instead of listening to the judgmental voices in our own heads. To see them as whole human beings and be excited for their ideas instead of trying to fix and "help" so much. Because it's in those little moments that John Gottman calls "sliding door moments" that we sew the fabric of trust, one little stitch at a time.

I want to live my life the way my grandfather did. To embrace each smile, each subtle gesture of connection, each little expression of love until it warms my heart instead of downplaying it, dismissing it, or hanging onto each snide remark or feeling of being unwanted or unappreciated. Because I know how easy it is to do that. And I know the pain it spreads, even if it feels good in the moment.

I want to love freely, without conditions attached to my love, because I know that when we start measuring, love stops flowing and fear creeps in. We gossip and we create little teams of "us" and "them," and, yes, this too feels good in the moment, because fault-finding fans a fragile ego. But we stay forever hungry or become demanding in our love. I don't want to be hungry anymore.

I once refused to starve my physical body. I now refuse to starve my soul.

Part 3

Building a Sense of Mastery

Chapter 6

Living with Purpose

"I want to find my purpose."

It's something that's bound to come up at some point in our coaching conversations. Often it is *the* reason clients enter the coaching relationship. "My job pays the bills, but I find no joy in it." Or "I've been in this career for ages, but I feel there's something more for me. Something else I'm being called to do. Except I don't know what it is."

Other times, it comes up as we do the work of belonging. It's as though clients are finally giving themselves permission to dig deeper, get in touch with their childhood dreams, and explore parts of themselves that bring them a greater sense of joy and meaning. We cannot do that when we place conditions on our worth.

Their longing for purpose tends to show up in one of three ways:

A *deep ache.* They talk about feelings of regret that keep them up at night or torment them through the day. Most times these regrets sound like, "If only I had taken that risk..." or what Daniel Pink calls *boldness regrets* in his book *The Power of Regret.*[58] At the heart of boldness regrets is playing it safe and not being true to ourselves. It's common in fragile confidence because putting our real selves out there is fraught with fear.

A sense of *dullness.* Some of them are already living full lives through their careers, families, or volunteering and community work. They may have a rich spiritual practice, where gratitude and mindfulness are daily practices that ground them. And yet they talk about something missing. Some call it joy. Others call it energy or creativity. They want a more *felt* experience of life, because we are, as French philosopher and paleontologist Pierre Teilhard de Chardon said, "spiritual beings having a human experience."[59]

An underlying *dissatisfaction.* Many of them feel disengaged from their work, even disillusioned by the choices they've made and the careers they've pursued, even though their jobs may be financially rewarding. Often, their choices reflect what Jonathan Gustin, founder of the Purpose Guides Institute, calls a "default purpose" that's based on other people's expectations or society's ideals of success.[60] They're tired, burned out, and searching for that something that brings them a deeper sense of meaning.

Even so, the search for purpose isn't easy because it's not your average conversation with yourself. **What is the work that brings me alive? What am I here to do with my life?** We've never really explored these questions. The world doesn't give us time to do so. Nor does it necessarily encourage them. The systems and structures we have in place need us to be a certain way, and they reward us for it.

When the silenced and suppressed parts of us speak up, we get thrown off because we don't know where to begin. Research shows that the search for purpose feels uplifting while we're still in our twenties. After that, there's a sense of dread and despair associated with it, which is why many of us give up when the answer isn't staring us in the face.

For starters, there's biological tendency; our hunter–gatherer ancestors had to find their purpose within the second and third decades of life, because their life expectancy wasn't what it is today. We carry the same brain atop our shoulders. When we don't find our purpose early on, we experience the existential loss of not having contributed to the world in a way that transcends our mortality.

There's also the social pressure to have found it *already*. These days, there's no end of books, stories, and examples of people who are living with purpose and experiencing joy and freedom beyond their wildest imaginations. Social media feeds overflow with images of gushing laughter and states of rapture, with captions that read: "Live with passion and abundance," "Release your divine feminine," and "Awaken your life of purpose." You feel like the only loser stuck in a meaningless job. Even if you thought you'd found your purpose, it certainly doesn't feel like those images. You wonder what's wrong with you.

There's nothing wrong with you. Purposeful work, *soul*ful work, is driven by the human quest for lasting meaning. And a life of meaning, the research shows, is less focused on *feeling* good and more on *doing* good. Its emotional state isn't necessarily positive all the time; in fact, happiness and meaning do not always go hand in hand. Ask anyone involved in raising a family or looking after aging parents, and they'll tell you about the challenges, the sleepless nights, and the self-sacrifices. Are they happy all the time? No. Are their lives free of worry and stress? No. Do they experience an enduring sense of meaning and fulfillment? Yes!

Purposeful work is soulful work. And as such, the conversation you need to have is with that something deep within that some call the soul, and others call the inner child. In essence, it is your authentic expression, your light in the world, your place of joy and purpose.

When we're little, we love to explore this place because we

have time, our creativity is boundless, and no one tells us it's wrong to do so. A three-year-old can enter a room and say with absolute conviction, "Look, Mama, I'm a fire truck!" And the next day invite you to ride with her in her rocket ship to the moon. Her imagination is trying out different garments and happy to let go of the ones that don't fit. Little girls can rest in this phase for longer because they're more attuned with their multiple selves and more sensitive to the sights and sounds of the world around us.

DISOWNING OURSELVES

I was ten when a family friend gifted me Louisa May Alcott's timeless classic *Little Women* for my birthday. As a somewhat introverted child with two vocal brothers and homeschooled in a foreign land, I immediately found an imaginary home with the four March sisters. Reading the book over and over again became a daily ritual. After a morning of tuition and activities, I would escape to the balcony outside my room and spend the entire afternoon reading the book as though for the first time. There was always more to imagine, and more to feel, until it was as though the sisters and I were joined together by an invisible umbilical cord.

By the time I'd emerge back into the house, it was usually dark. The warmth of late-afternoon light still lingered in the bedroom I shared with Dadima. It was time to change and hurry down for dinner, where my dad would inquire about our day and talk about our homework for the next day. If he had time, he'd introduce a topic of current affairs for my brothers and me to debate.

I didn't like debate nights. My older brother read the daily newspaper and was far more knowledgeable than me. My younger brother had spunk and the ability to convince others of (often incorrect) facts simply by being overly confident about them. I'd tried to develop both qualities—a love of facts and a quick wit—and failed because I was trying to be someone I wasn't.

In my imaginary world, I was free to be me. I was free to explore and enjoy the whole of me. Some days, I had Jo's high-spiritedness, her keen observation, and her love of words. Other days, I basked in the limelight with Amy's air of self-importance. And almost always, I felt drawn to Beth's soft-spoken manner. No one judged me, no one compared me, no one expected me to be a certain "right" way. Much less my own mind.

I never shared this imaginary world with anyone. I feared my brothers would double up in fits of laughter, or my parents would suggest expanding my literary prowess over my imaginary one. But there was also the fear of my world losing its magic if it were exposed. It felt too precious, too tender to face the thoughts and opinions of a world that seemed at odds with the joys and longings of the soul.

So I tucked it away, as most of us do. I turned to the world to tell me how to be and what to do, again as most of us do. And layer by layer, the world douses the flames of our inner world and replaces it with enough objections that we begin doubting it ourselves.

Education trains us in logic and reason. Our dreams lose their power because we stop speaking their language of images, intuitions, and bodily sensations. Our passions are sidelined because they're not practical enough—"Art won't make you rich," or "Making jewelry is a nice hobby." And our visions for a better world are deemed too extreme or "idealistic": "Like c'mon, you think you can actually bring clean water to Africa?"

There are other blows too that are carefully reserved for women and girls. Very early on, we learn to suppress our ambitions because we're primed to believe that men can go after their dreams while women need to be the caregivers. On the very first call of a recent Goodbye Perfect Program cohort, a participant said: "I'm tired of being the matriarch of the family. I never married; I don't have children. All my life I've been raising my brothers and my nephews and nieces, and I want to be done with that. I want to live my life. I'm sixty-four now. When will it be my turn?"

There's also the harsh disowning of our bodies because a woman's sexuality has always threatened the male ego. Starting in adolescence, and sometimes even earlier, we receive insidious messages of how to curb our sexuality and fix parts of us that proclaim our power. I grew up in a part of the world where patriarchy is both undisguised and unapologetic. A visit to the bazaar (markets that sell everything from cloth to spices to precious stones) would often feel like a journey through a battle zone. Make sure you're twice covered over with chadars. Make sure you avoid the gaze and ignore the ogles of idle men and shopkeepers. Make sure you hide the very existence of your breasts and bottoms because men shouldn't have to take responsibility for their behaviors.

Even in post-MeToo societies, women carry the same shame around their bodies because patriarchy has been the world order for millennia. We fix, hide, torture, starve, even put under the scalpel parts of us that have carried babies and that have fed and rocked them. When we reject our bodies, we cannot access our souls, because the soul is housed within the body. It's one of the few good lessons ED taught me.

When we lose touch with important aspects of who we are—our body, our intuition, our dreams, desires, and sources of joy and creativity—we lock the door on our lives and hand over the key to others. **We become an object of external demands, and not the subject of our own lives.**

Even the entire concept of autonomy can baloney for women;

without connection to our deepest truth, our choices are often a reflection of the societies we live in, even though we believe they're internally generated. Sometimes, the permission to "be anything you want to be" is our greatest source of suffering, because our pursuits leave us feeling empty. We are accomplices in the construction of a self that doesn't serve us, with the added pain of believing we created her ourselves.

COMING BACK HOME

Is it any wonder that most of us arrive at the gates of mid-adulthood, strangers to ourselves? We look at ourselves and wonder how we became this way. There's sadness, perhaps regrets. And there's confusion. *Who am I? What do I want? How did I even get here?*

Whoever you are and however you got here, rest assured that you're exactly where you need to be. There's a deep relaxing that comes with this knowing. An undoing of the stresses of being behind, of comparison, of feeling like you wasted your life. The long and winding journey of disconnect is one we all go through. Some of us wander farther away because of our personal experiences. And for women in particular, the labyrinth is an unspoken rite of passage into womanhood.

But now, you're done growing older and it's time to grow up. Your spiritual journey has begun. And this journey, writes Franciscan priest Richard Rohr in his book *Falling Upward*, has two parts.[61] The first is about re-finding your true nature. The second is about living it, perhaps an even harder task, and yet the most essential. Research on meaning by Michael Steger at Colorado State University shows that finding purpose *but not living it* is a source of even greater angst and loss of confidence because it's now fueled by regrets.

"What a man can be, he must be," wrote Abraham Maslow of self-actualization.[62] What follows in this chapter is a guide to both parts of the spiritual journey.

FINDING PURPOSE

I like to think of the journey within as deep-sea diving for two reasons. One, it's apt imagery—we go deeper and deeper, beyond the world as we know it, beyond our conscious fears and beliefs, and come face-to-face with hidden beliefs and the bigger fears of death and impermanence. At the same time, we begin to witness the divinity reflected in every new leaf and creature, and see ourselves as part of a much larger, much more glorious world. Such is the soul—deep, dark, magical, paradoxical, interconnected, and insanely abundant.

It's also a reminder of how the soul communicates with us—through imagery and bodily sensations, through whispers and inaudible sounds, much like the sea-world. When we listen with only our heads, we miss all the other messages that point us to our life's callings. And when we listen from the whole of us—from our bodies and our hearts, we feel the pangs of conscience or discontent. We hear the murmurs of inspiration, the twinges of intuition, the little jolts of insight.

When you begin to feel like a fish out of water, spend some time in silence and solitude. Ask yourself the questions, and then listen. Truly listen. Listen with your body, like you would listen to a piece of music. Listen to images, bodily sensations, or a feeling and knowing that's difficult to explain because there's no logic behind it.

If you hear yourself say, "I don't have time to listen," recognize it as the harried voice of your inner manager—remember her from chapter 4? She wants to make sure the pain from the past doesn't flood your conscious awareness. And so she pesters you to perfect, control, fix, and stay busy, usually in not so important work. Let her know *this* is important work. Her stuff can wait.

As you listen, do not force an answer. The longing for an answer kills the question, because the soul is wary. She is like a wild animal, writes author and activist Parker Palmer in his book *A Hidden Wholeness*: "tough, resilient, savvy, self-sufficient and yet exceedingly shy."[63] She is your inner child—perhaps exiled—and needs time to reveal herself. And every parent knows that if you want the truth, you cannot force your scared child to speak. You simply hold the silence like a precious little seedling waiting to be born. And you wait.

You wait until thoughts of social obligations and constraints die down. You wait until what someone said or did no longer occupies your mind. Until the inner critics and ghosts of the past step back. Even your own ideas of what you want fade away. As you separate yourself from others and from the world, you begin to see more clearly what distinguishes you from them. You see your strengths, your gifts, and what kind of person you are.

And that's where the magic of solitude happens. The more you separate yourself, the more you realize your connection with the world. As Buddhist scholar Stephen Batchelor writes, "Look long and hard enough at yourself in isolation and suddenly you will see the rest of humanity staring back."[64]

This is the essence of purpose—it doesn't exist in isolation because the soul belongs to the larger flow of life. Each of us comes into the world to make it a little better in some small way. And in doing so, we find joy, success and fulfillment. Such is the wisdom of the universe.

In Shamanism, one of the most ancient healing traditions to exist, purpose is our medicine, our unique way of bringing healing into the world. In their worldview, the natural world has it too; for example, some trees have medicinal properties, while others provide shade. Some are a home for certain birds and others exist simply to bring beauty and wonder into the world. In humans, purpose also has the element of joy—writer Frederick

Buechner, describes it as "the place where your deep gladness and the world's deep hunger meet."[37]

An understanding of purpose as a two-way street also debunks one of the greatest myths that holds many people back from living a purposeful life. We tend to believe that each of us comes into the world with that *one* purpose that's our contribution to the world and our path to fulfillment. I've seen so many women caught in a state of limbo, because if there's only one right path, it places enormous pressure to get it right. There's confusion, there's paralysis by analysis, and there's the waiting that happens when you aren't ready to settle for anything less than perfect. Author Patrick McGinnis, who coined the term *FOMO* (fear of missing out and has written a book by the same name), calls it *FOBO*: the fear of a better option. And it leaves behind a trail of frustrations and regrets.

Healing, by definition, exists in relationship to the needs around us. And this means that our purpose can change and evolve depending on our circumstances. This is particularly helpful for women because we go through so many transitions in life where we're called to redefine ourselves in new and purposeful ways. Time and again, I hear women talk about the need to find "me" again, once children are born, or grow older or leave home. Or when a parent or in-law needs caregiving and they are the only ones who can provide it. Recently, a client came to do the work of purpose because her partner had passed away and she was now the sole breadwinner.

The concept of an evolving purpose can also help us stay engaged and do our best work in a world where change is the only constant. Most of us will likely go through multiple career changes in life, needing to redefine ourselves to meet new opportunities when old ones become less rewarding, get outsourced, or give way to automation. Unless we can sift through our inner sea to find what feels joyful and meaningful at this time, we'll end up feeling bitter, disadvantaged, unable to adapt to life's winds, or to answer the call of the moment.

One of the most pressing calls these days is to turn toward the needs of our struggling world. It's being felt not only by those of us of a certain age, but also by the younger population still in the process of deciding or reflecting on their career paths. "I want to make a meaningful difference in the world," they say. My friend's twenty-two-year-old son just gave up his dream of becoming a rich investment banker because he found it "soulless."

Soulful work indeed makes a difference because the soul follows a different timeline. Its perspective is long, which gives us the patience to wait and to face disappointments with grace when our efforts do not pay off immediately. It allows us to plant the seeds of a better tomorrow, trusting that one day they will blossom, even if we don't live to see it in our lifetime.

DIVING DEEP IN

When you start feeling something is missing, it's time to take the deep dive within to find who or what's calling you right now. And how can you meet their needs in the most joyful way?

Here are a few common patterns to watch out for. Even if none of them speak to you, you'll have started the most important conversation of your life.

A Pain or Frustration

You feel angered by, frustrated about, or tired of a lack in some aspect of your work, home, or community life that you feel called to correct. You may not quite know what you will do about it or even have a vision of a better alternative. But you're deeply aware of the pain, the inefficiencies, or simply the inconvenience or irritation in the way things are.

This is one of the most common ways of finding our purpose, because negative emotions are powerful in driving action. So many innovations and advancements have roots in a frustration; Uber began on a snowy night in Paris when the two founders were stranded in the cold after a conference because all the taxis in the city were taken. And Rosa Parks's refusal to give up her seat to a white passenger on the bus was a result of a tiredness she described in her 1992 autobiography, *Rosa Parks: My Story*: "People always say that I didn't give up my seat because I was tired, but that isn't true. I was not tired physically, or no more tired than I usually was at the end of a working day. I was not old, although some people have an image of me as being old then. I was forty-two. No, the only tired I was, was tired of giving in."[65]

A Sense of Responsibility

You have a feeling that a certain work is yours to do. It may be because you've lived through a certain experience, perhaps an accident you had, and you decided to become a motivational speaker. Or having a child with special needs made you commit yourself to raising awareness and funds to treat their condition.

It could also be a feeling you've always had for no particular reason. Rosie, whom I got to know through the Goodbye Perfect Project, was a live-in caregiver to a young boy on the extreme end of the autism spectrum. In one of our sessions, she spoke about the challenges of her job: "He doesn't sleep much and paces the room all night. I have to keep following him so he doesn't hurt himself. He's also becoming bigger, and I'm afraid he'll hurt me because he pushes me and hits me sometimes."

I asked her whether she'd thought of finding another job. "I can't," she said firmly. "God sent me to do this work. Until it is done, I have to stay." The spiritual meaning was the force that kept her committed to a physically challenging job. For her, it was a calling, and it brought her a sense of peace and meaning.

An Uplifting Vision

You see a gap in the way things are and are drawn by a mental image of something better. Something in you has an idea of how to make it more efficient, more beautiful, more beneficial in some way. Something in you says, "I can make it better." Usually, an uplifting vision is tied to our passions or areas of strength, which is why it excites us.

A few months ago, a friend organized cooking classes on Zoom, run by Syrian refugee women who were living in camps on the Turkish border. She was drawn to the idea of helping women use their existing skills to make lives better for their families. And she chose cooking because it's been a passion of hers ever since she was little.

An uplifting vision can also show up as a love for gardening, art, music, or jewelry-making, because beauty is a uniquely human endeavor. A dog doesn't dream of a better kennel (or so we think), but humans dream of the architecture that they go on to build, and the bands that then travel to small towns to bring love and laughter to struggling lives. They have a vision of something that excites them or makes them feel happy, hopeful, or empowered. The vision doesn't have to be crystal clear—it may be fleeting images of love, laughter, or a sense of a peaceful ecology. Or it may be something concrete like a business that sells products made from seashells or a traveling band that visits small towns in East Africa.

An Enduring Dream

You've always had a vision of who you want to be. It could be the answer you gave as a little child to that question adults invariably ask: "Who do you want to be when you grow up?" It could come from what others, especially people who knew you well, said to you: "I see you as someone who would love working with little children."

Or it could be a vision that you have for no particular reason. Margie, the receptionist at my dentist's office, once said to me: "I've this very powerful vision of standing in front of lots and lots of people. And I'm dressed in a suit and I'm educating them. I don't know where it comes from. I've never worn a suit or given a lecture. But something tells me I can do it. It excites me."

If you don't have a vision yet, you can start thinking about your life in the future if everything were to go your way. What's the work you're doing? Who are the people you're impacting? Why does the work feel meaningful? If fears come up, extend your timeline ten or even twenty years from now. Fear is much more vocal when action is imminent.

You can think about the legacy you want to leave behind. It sounds a little morbid I know, but thinking about death can help us focus on what's important in life. Through the centuries, almost every civilization has had its forms of "memento mori"— reminders of the inevitability of death in order to live life fully.

Think about what you want people to say about you in your obituary or at your funeral. What would you regret not doing in your life? Why?

A Feeling of Flow

You feel energized, uplifted, and in charge. You're brimming with ideas, you find it easy to reach out to others, and when challenges come up, you look for ways to overcome them. It may not be fun and games all the time, but there's a sense of possibility even in the struggle.

Research on the state of "flow" shows that in these moments, you're at your most authentic because there's an absence of self-consciousness.[66] You're doing what you naturally do best, whether it's perspective-taking, leadership, gratitude, or creativity.

You can also find your strengths by taking a psychometric test, which is common practice in most organizations. But unless you think of times you used these strengths, and see them *in action*, you will neither own them nor know how to use them effectively. Overuse and underuse of strengths happens all the time, especially in fragile confidence. Overuse leads to burnout, feelings of being unappreciated, and things not going well despite massive effort. Underuse shows up as procrastination, lack of confidence, and a nagging fear of failure.

Feeling Inspired

You look at other people's lives and feel inspired in some way. It could be the work they're doing or the way they make others feel around them. It could be the energy with which they show up every day or the way they deal with challenges that touches upon your core values. If you look at someone and think *I want to be like that*, you've tapped into that bigger version of you that you know is possible.

I remember Kathryn who came to me because she felt guilty about her role as a mother. "I have a job I love," she said, "but whenever I'm working, I keep telling myself I should be with my daughter who is a special needs child." When we did the work around values, she shared how her maternal aunt had been her greatest source of inspiration. "She had eight children," she said. "But she knew how to make each one of them feel special."

Kathryn started making small changes in her life so she could give her full attention to her daughter when they were together. Today, she runs a small school for special needs children with a 1:2 ratio of teacher to child. She found her purpose by being inspired by her aunt's life.

Childhood Memories

When you think back to your childhood, you remember places or images that spoke to you, or perhaps still do. I remember when

I was little, I used to be mesmerized by the windows of houses when we drove through the streets of Colombo (Sri Lanka). It wasn't easy seeing the windows because the streets were lined with lush trees. But I would always try, because those windows allowed me to imagine life inside the houses.

One day, not long after I began my coaching work, I was thinking about that particular childhood memory. And it dawned on me that my work as a coach wasn't much different. I helped women look through the windows into their inner world. The memory didn't reveal my path in life, but it had made my existing work far more purposeful. I experienced a heightened energy, a strong desire to make a bigger impact. Ideas flowed. And this book was one of them.

Inner Work

You know that you are carrying resentments, fears, shame, or guilt that you need to work through before you can show up in the world in any substantial way. For most of us, this work happens in tandem with the work out in the real world, because healing ourselves is work we all need to do.

Sometimes though, this work itself is our calling in the moment because it needs the whole of us to work through it. There was no way I could work through the deepest waters of my eating disorder while also attending school, fixing the relationships that had been affected, and pursing my creative interests. My purpose then was my inner work. It was recovering myself enough to know what was getting in the way of me being more empowered, more free, more loving, more comfortable setting boundaries or accepting people's boundaries.

If this is what speaks to you right now, you may want to begin by writing down all the resentments, all the fears, and all the things you feel shame about. And then to look at the list and see which one has the greatest pull force. That's where you begin.

NOT KNOWING

It's possible that none of these reflections bring up much for you. And that's okay! It doesn't mean you'll never find your purpose, or that you don't have one. You just need to dig a little deeper.

According to a Hindu myth that I heard a long time ago, the gods decided to hide our purpose deep within us because they figured that's where we'll stop looking, if we ever do. Now that you've started, keep looking until you find it. Here are a few ways to continue the search:

Experimenting

Listening inward does not have to be a solitary pursuit. The moments that most speak to us don't always happen on the meditation cushion but off it, in our encounters with the real world. It makes sense because the soul finds inspiration in interconnectedness.

You can begin by experimenting with passions or interests you once had. If you loved dancing as a little girl, go back and see whether your older self finds something purposeful in it. I remember a client who noticed that many of the women in her dance class were using movement as a way to heal from trauma. She began studying about psychosomatic approaches to healing, and now has her own dance school for women who suffered emotional abuse in their intimate relationships.

Journaling

Journaling is another great way to get in touch with your inner world. Set aside time every day to write—no planning, no editing. Simply ask yourself *What do I want to do with my life?* and write *straight* for about fifteen to twenty minutes. If you can't think of what to write, simply write "I cannot think of what to write..." and keep writing whatever comes up, even if it looks like gibberish.

If you want a slightly more structured approach, reflect on your day. Write about what you did or who you met. How did you feel? What touched you in some way? Why? What did you like or not like? What made you feel alive? What would you like to explore more of? How will you do so?

Talking

Sometimes simply talking to others and having them reflect back the qualities they see in you can help in identifying or accepting what you're too scared to own in yourself. Both in my earlier therapy practice, and in my current coaching practice, I've seen women transform simply through the conversations we have in the safe container of a trusting relationship.

The person you choose to talk to needs to be someone who holds you in "unconditional positive regard"—meaning no judgment, no correcting, no pretending they know what is right for you. According to Carl Rogers, this is a key quality that helps people reach their highest potential.

Prayer

I personally love this one, not just for finding purpose, but for any challenge that exceeds our ability to make sense if it. Prayer not only moves us out of our heads, it also transports us to a place of receptivity to whatever comes up.

You do not have to pray to a god or gods if religion is not your thing. Prayer can be to any larger force that speaks to the spiritual aspect of being human. You can direct your prayer to the universe or to "the forces out there." Or you can simply spend time in nature and allow the magnitude of it all to awaken something in you.

RESISTING PURPOSE

It's enticing to believe that once we know what's calling us, we'll experience an unstoppable urge to run with it. In my experience, both personal and professional, I've found that what we experience is the opposite—fear, doubts, and a longing for the comfort of our old lives.

It is important to understand this how this fear shows up, because it's different to the fear instinct that's part of our evolutionary inheritance (which we'll address in the next chapter). The fear we feel when we think about our purpose is more like the emotion of **awe**. Awe is the feeling of being in the presence of the divine or of something so vast that it transcends our understanding of the world. We feel awe looking up at the stars in the night sky, standing beneath tall trees as the sun shines through, watching a little child give her food to a stranger, or witnessing a baby being born into the world.

We feel the same emotion when we see something *in us* that takes our breath away. But instead of experiencing the wonder and curiosity that is commonly associated with awe, many of us experience awe's lesser-known effect: dread.[67] The kind of dread we feel when we witness nature's capacity for destruction (hurricanes, pandemics, etc.) and instinctively run for our lives.

Here's how author and spiritual leader Marianne Williamson describes this fear in her bestselling book *A Return to Love*: "Our deepest fear is not that we are inadequate. Our deepest fear is that we are powerful beyond measure. It is our light, not our darkness, that most frightens us. We ask ourselves, *Who am I to be brilliant, gorgeous, talented, fabulous?*"[68]

So why does awe show up as dread and not curiosity? Because in fragile confidence, the inner firefighter we met back in chapter 4 sees brokenness and not brilliance. Where there's potential, she sees pain. Where there's light, she sees lack. When the exiled inner child demands self-expression, she'll do everything in her power to tamp it down and muffle its voice.

Here are some of the common objections I've heard from women when we do the work around purpose:

Objection #1: "But this isn't much."

Sometimes, clients don't like the callings they receive because they feel frivolous, small, or not noble enough. Or they feel too easy or fun, and as high-achieving women used to proving themselves, they reject anything that doesn't involve blood, toil, tears, and sweat.

If this is you, trust that callings are always in answer to your best contribution and in proportion to the resources you currently have to meet them. Maybe at this stage in your life, this is what most excites you or the best you can manage. Your ego will need to accept that.

Objection #2: "But others are already doing it."

This is the client who wants her work to take the world by storm, who still wears the Superwoman cloak. If others are already doing it, it is no longer special in the way the ego wants it to be.

If this is you, trust that soulful work always happens in collaboration. Once you fully own your strengths, you'll appreciate the value that only *you* can bring to the work. The "others" are not threats but kindred spirits on a common journey who can help augment the work so it has an even bigger impact in the world.

Objection #3: "Me? But I'm so flawed myself."

A personal attack is the firefighter's favorite way of shutting us down. And it usually works, because we all have flaws and weaknesses. When we do not accept these flaws as part of being human, it's easy to turn away from the calling.

If this is you, trust that callings come our way to stretch us, to heal us, and to help us grow and become a better version of ourselves. Personal growth is like an asymptote—you'll keep moving closer and closer to your ideal, but the work is never fully done.

Objection #4: "But I don't have the skills."

This is similar to the previous objection, except it's directed at competence. Again, some of it may be true. But when we are trying to prove ourselves through our competence, we keep gathering more and more qualifications instead of actually doing the work.

If this is you, trust that you likely have all the qualifications you need *to begin*. You may need more down the road, but before you enroll in a certification program or a two-year degree, listen for enough real evidence that you need to do so. Callings come to us for many reasons, and having the right qualifications is just one of them.

Objection #5: "But I'm not ready."

Another version of the same objection, this is the all-time favorite of the perfectionist and keeps us in perpetual waiting mode. We keep planning and strategizing and making sure everything is perfect before we begin.

If this is you, trust that you are more ready than you feel. Put your incomplete course out there, press Publish on your blog, reach out to the TEDx organizers, or apply for that job that excites you. Begin before you *feel* ready because planning is never a substitute for the learning that happens along the way.

Objection #6: "But my kids will suffer."

Yet another version of the previous objections, this one hits the "mom guilt" nerve, which is always vigilant for signs we've messed our kids up in some way. Women can spend their entire lives "in waiting," because children's needs rarely come to a full stop.

If this is you, trust that children, once past their very early years, are tougher, more resilient, and more self-sufficient than you think. If they're still little, your calling may be to tend to them right now. But callings change, remember, and maybe it's time you moved on.

Objection #7: "But there's no money in it."

This is one of the most common objections I get in my conversations around purpose. And it's a legitimate one. If we have to choose, our basic needs of food and shelter will always trump the higher needs for purpose and meaning. We're made for physical survival.

If this is you, trust that soulful work never promised to pay the bills. It may, but it's rare for a calling to also be our source of income. Much more on this in the section on Integrating Purpose.

Objection #8: "But it's too big."

When callings feel big, the fear of failure can be debilitating, because we feel small in comparison. The fear is even stronger in anxious attachment where feelings of inadequacy can be quite vocal.

If this is you, trust that your calling is within your capacity to answer it. Become aware of the resources you already have that are sometimes easy to overlook—time, money, relationships, qualifications, a certain awareness or strength that will help you meet it. Think of how you've risen to challenges in the past and what helped you do so.

Objection #9: "But it isn't even clear."

This is a classic fear giveaway. Fear can't deal with ambiguity and uncertainty because it doesn't have rules for them. And yet, lack of clarity often points to a calling because the soul speaks to us through imagery and whispers and bodily sensations.

If this is you, trust that the search for clarity is the search for safety. And when there's nothing to fear but fear itself, you need to listen to the gentle stirrings of your heart. The clarity you seek will emerge in the process of honoring your calling.

Objection #10: "But Mom wouldn't approve."

Of course, the approval card! If it isn't Mom, it's friends, family, kids, or a partner. Or it could be colleagues or society at large. One of my dentist clients felt a real call to pivot to a coaching career but kept obsessing about what others would think: "How do I tell people I'm starting a coaching business? They'll think I'm wasting my qualification."

If this is you, trust that the *only* people you need to consider for your calling are the recipients of your work. Not your mom or friends or online followers. Not how it will look on your résumé or your social media profile. Their input, however well meant, is disconnected with your soul.

Objection #11: "But it sounds so selfish."

Unless the calling is evidently selfless, many women can feel guilty about following it. This is yet another way gender socialization shows up in our lives—we're worthy only as long as we are living for others.

If this is you, trust that the only selfish thing you can do with your calling is to dismiss it. Remember, your purpose was never meant for you—it's there to help and heal the world. Your calling is an invitation to do so. Accept it.

Objection #12: "But I don't have the time."

This is another very common objection, especially if we're at a stage of life when we're pulled in many different directions. How can I possibly find time for what lights me up when there's so much to do and so many responsibilities to fulfill?

If this is you, trust that soulful work simply needs to be expressed in the world. How much time you spend doing it is of least concern because it is disconnected with notions of time. More on this in the Integrating Purpose section.

EMBRACING PURPOSE

The reality is that **soulful work is work we receive**. We don't choose it. We don't assess it. We don't argue with it. The head has no say in matters of the soul. Some of us go through our entire lives feeling justified in listening to our objections. But there *will* come a time when the soul finally makes itself heard. It's been keeping score. It has noted every time you let it down, denied its voice, shied away from its call. It's noted every time you gave in to your fears and stepped back into the false safety of your unlived life. And it feels cheated by you.

So put your objections away and embrace the purpose you've been given. Accept it with open arms and bow your head down in gratitude. The gratitude of a receiver who has been gifted something beautiful. Something magical. Something divine, because your purpose was placed within you in the moment of conception. As the Persian poet Hafiz says:

> *This place where you are now*
> *God circled on a map for you.*[69]

When you step fully into the circle, the universe will celebrate you wholeheartedly, the way the jungle celebrated Simba in the *Lion King* when he accepted his place in the circle of life. You have accepted your part toward the healing and happiness of the universe, and it will now work for you. This is the foundational philosophy of Paulo Coelho's *The Alchemist*: "When you really want something, it's because that desire originated in the soul of the universe...the whole universe conspires in order for you to achieve it."[70]

Doors will open and abundance will flow in. People you could've never imagined will enter your life, eager to help. Some days, it'll feel like you're walking on a cloud because your heart is so happy. Other days, you'll feel that it's not you, but a force flowing through you. That you're the tap and not the water.

In reality, you're both. It's what the second half of the spiritual life is all about—coming up next.

LIVING WITH PURPOSE

One of the key challenges in this second half of the spiritual journey—especially for women—is that our roles and responsibilities never quite end. We continue to be caregivers or bread-earners. We continue to expand our areas of engagement and influence, all of which take time and energy. Time and energy away from the purpose that we've worked hard to find. It seems we have only three choices: wait for the "right" time, leave our current work (however we define it) in pursuit of our purpose. Or try and have it all, because anything less is not acceptable to a mind raised on a steady diet of perfection.

All these choices deny an inherent fact of our humanity. We're each many "selves," and a well-lived life is less about having it all, and more about honoring them all. In her beautiful piece titled "Of Power and Time," Mary Oliver identifies two key selves: the social self and the creative self. The social self, she writes, lives in the real world and is "fettered to a thousand notions of obligation."[71] She's the one who remembers doctors' appointments, makes sure homework gets done, and stays up to complete the unfinished slide deck. Women's social selves take up a huge chunk of our lives given the many roles we play.

The "creative self," on the other hand, lives *beyond* the real world. It doesn't care if the laundry gets done or if our boss praises our ideas. But it does care, very deeply, about our purpose because "it has a hunger for eternity." The social self makes the world go around. The creative self moves the world forward, because it isn't bound to social norms and expectations.

It was my creative self who offered Zoom gatherings to hundreds of women when the world shut down in the early days of the pandemic, even though I'd just lost three premolars and there was a huge gap on the upper left side of my mouth. The kids were aghast and wondered whether I'd also lost a bit of my mind. My social self panicked. Would people think the same? Would they laugh? Should I wait until I'd filled the gap?

My creative self refused to wait. My purpose in that moment was loud and clear. Teeth didn't matter.

In our everyday lives, though, they do matter. We do, after all, live in the real world. To live a purpose-driven life, we have to integrate the creative self into our ordinary lives, with our ordinary concerns, roles, and responsibilities. This is *feminine* spirituality—not either or, not black and white, not all or nothing. As Mirabai Starr, author of *Wild Mercy* explains, it is **both-and**, because it is underpinned by the matriarchal acceptance and union of paradox.[72] It is not life in a dojo, nor sailing above our emotional lives. It is about being connected in empathic bonds with the whole of who we are, so we can say *yes!* to a purpose-driven life even while doing the dishes, earning a living, or holding space for your difficult teenager.

Here are three ways of doing so:

As part of: You can create purpose within your work or any task you do or role you play by bringing your strengths, passions, and motivations to it. This can take a couple of forms. If your calling is to send your kids to a private college, you can engage in a soulless-but-well-paying job as the gateway to your purpose. If it is to make people feel valued and worthy, you can listen more deeply or take a genuine interest in people's goals and aspirations. Purpose is less about what you do and more about how you do it.

You can also substitute some of your current tasks with what feels more authentic and meaningful. This is called "job crafting," a widely researched concept first introduced by Amy Wrzesniewski and Jane Dutton in 2001. The purpose is to "craft" a job—a relationship, a task, or a perspective—so it's aligned with how you work best, where you can contribute the most and what you feel most called to do.

An understanding of purpose as "part of" is also hugely helpful in organizations, because many leaders believe that if they were to help their employees find their purpose, they would leave. Quite the contrary; research shows that job crafting leads to greater engagement, job satisfaction, and motivation.

Separate from: If your work doesn't allow this kind of flexibility, you can do purpose work on the side, as a hobby, a passion project, or as community or mentorship work. This idea can sometimes sound unappealing. I've had clients say, "But shouldn't my purpose be central to my life?" Not really. Purpose doesn't care how many hours you devote to it or how much space it occupies in your life. Time and again, I've seen clients find incredible joy from simply spending a couple of hours a week doing their art, helping out in a soup kitchen, or whatever else is calling them at that stage in their lives.

Instead of: Only a very few of us are able to turn our purpose into a full-time career. If you're contemplating this route, make sure it's not a hasty decision. Have you saved enough to sustain yourself until your pursuit bears financial fruits? Do you have a plan for the unexpected and resources you will lean on when it happens?

It's a big decision, so take your time. Talk to people. Is what you're contemplating the only way you can express your purpose? Experiment to see whether you truly find the joy and fulfillment you think you will. Too often, I've seen women get hung up on a certain idea and end up with both emotional pain and financial fallouts.

Zara was in her late fifties and in a role at a nonprofit organization that paid well and had great benefits, but it was not aligned with the work she most wanted to do. She figured a master's degree in social policy would help her find a job that was a better fit and enrolled in a demanding program that she pursued after work.

When Zara came to me, she was feeling burned out and guilty that she wasn't fully there for her twenty-three-year-old daughter who had been in and out of rehab twice. She'd also begun to doubt whether the degree would actually help her find the job she wanted and whether it would provide her with the same pay and benefits she currently had, which were important to her.

I suggested looking at alternate ways of meeting her purpose—community work, involvement in grassroots efforts, starting a weekly blog to raise awareness on issues that were important to her. She struggled with the idea. "I don't think that's enough," she said. I suggested she try it, because her life didn't hold space for much more at the time. To her surprise, she found her side projects to be just as fulfilling.

Debbie, on the other hand, was completely on board with a more flexible approach to a purpose-driven life. She was a nonequity partner at a boutique law firm, and given her own experience, she knew that her calling was to help people in high-stress jobs manage their emotions through yoga and mindfulness practices. "I can't do it full time," she said. "I need to save for my sons' private education, and my job is the fastest way to do so. I also love what I do and want to be made full partner."

She rented a studio near her home and began offering Sunday morning yoga classes at no charge. Initially, it was just the colleagues at her small firm who attended, because she had no time to spread the word. But word got around nonetheless, and within a few months, she had over fifty people at each session. Seeing the need, she hired a couple of instructors and offered more classes. She also began charging a small fee to cover her expenses. By the time she was made partner a couple of years later, the practice had grown enough to become her full-time job. She has now expanded to other cities in her native UK.

LIVING WITH EASE

The Greek mathematician and astronomer Archimedes is thought to have said, "Give me a place to stand and a lever long enough, and I will move the world."[73] Purpose gives us a place to stand. But often, we burn ourselves out because we haven't created enough distance from the noise of the world. Our levers are too short.

We start perfecting, proving, performing, and comparing because the inner manager, who is heavily keyed in on societal standards, takes over the reins. *Who's doing what? What does the internet say about how to increase my following? How do I turn my purpose into a six-figure job?*

Even our most soulful goals can turn into "should" goals when we're not careful *how* we approach them. Greg McKeown, also known as the "Father of Essentialism," shares the experiences that led to his second book, *Effortless*. Even though he had trimmed his life down to the bare essentials, he found that he had no room to maneuver when life threw curve balls. *"I was doing all the right things for the right reasons. But I was doing them in the wrong way."*[74]

The right way, he found, was in taking the easiest path to the right things. This isn't easy (no pun intended) in a society that's based on the puritan idea—rooted in patriarchy—that there's inherent value in hard work. I'm not against hard work. In fact, I cringe every time I hear the people say something like *"No one ever lay on their deathbed wishing they'd worked harder."* It's likely true for people who spent their lives doing work that wasn't aligned with their deepest joys and callings. But it denies the inherent fulfillment human beings find in adding value through hard work, whether it's in the context of a job, relationships, or parenting.

The problem with the idea of hard work as it's currently understood is that it mistrusts the matriarchal approach of listening to our body and respecting its needs of rest and renewal. We weren't made to run endlessly, any more than a deer is capable of boundless escape or a lion of perpetual hunting. Research on peak performance at the Johnson & Johnson Human Performance Institute likens life to a set of sprints, not a marathon. If we don't listen to what we need, or get caught up in what others are doing, we expend too much energy and, sooner or later, burn ourselves out.

The importance of listening in and keeping a safe distance from the noise of the world cannot be overstated in a world of eight billion people and growing, no end of options to choose from, and perpetual innovation. However hard we try, we'll always feel behind. When I talk to young girls in high school, I'm pained to see that they have no time in their lives for relaxation, nor are they happy with the fruits of their efforts. "I can't go home with a ninety on my math paper!" "How will I ever get into college with only three APs?" They don't even have time to learn tools to manage their anxiety. Stress and burnout are an epidemic that has no age barriers.

If you're procrastinating or feeling unmotivated or overwhelmed in the pursuit of your goals or by the task of living a purposeful life, it's a sign that you aren't looking after yourself. You haven't built structures of ease into your life. You aren't taking care of the container that can hold the contents and contradictions of your mind and life.

In a 1988 interview with Bill Moyers on the television series *The Power of Myth*, mythologist Joseph Campbell spoke about the importance of taking care of ourselves in order for our light to shine through. "Am I the bulb that carries the light, or am I the light of which the bulb is a vehicle?" he said, affirming that we are, in fact, both.[75]

For your light to have the greatest impact, you need to look after the bulb as best as you can. This is where the inner dream-maker comes in.

THE INNER DREAM-MAKER

Who is an inner dream-maker? She is the inner presence who believes in your dreams and protects them from the noise, challenges, and setbacks. Think of her as the parent that Kahlil Gibran addresses in his beautiful poem "On Children":

> *You are the bows from which your children*
> *As living arrows are sent forth.*[76]

She doesn't decide your purpose, but she will bend over backward to make sure you live it well. She sees your passion for creative work and signs you up for art class. She knows your vision to go into diplomacy and cradles it until you're ready. She watches you struggle with time or energy, with self-criticism or blame and negativity. And she helps you take charge of what you put into your body, mind, and life so you're showing up in your full power, instead of driving on an empty engine, or with the brakes on.

Best of all, she doesn't push, pester, or pressure you to make it happen. Instead, like most parents, she sets structures in place that help you honor the many aspects of your paradoxical life.

This is crucial in a world that isn't made for our flourishing. More and more, we're struggling to take care of our basic needs without feeling like an eccentric, to open up to joy and wonder without feeling it's a waste of time, or to silence the voices that demand perfection and the endless pursuit for more. More and more, we need structures in our lives that optimize our energy so we stay on top of our game.

In his book *The Power of Full Engagement*, performance psychologist Jim Loehr explains energy as a triangle with four layers.[77] Spiritual energy, he states, sits atop three layers where physical energy is at the bottom, followed by emotional and then mental energy. Ask yourself: **What helps me have a good day? What helps me feel vital and alive?** And then go over the questions related to each level of energy and set your day up for success. Because as author Annie Dillard said: "How we spend our days is, of course, how we spend our lives."[78]

Level 1: Physical energy:

How will I bookend my day—what time will I wake up and when will I go to bed? When will I start work / end work?

What changes will I make to my diet?

What forms of movement will I include in my day?

Level 2: Emotional energy:

What thoughts will I stay away from (comparison, negativity, cynicism, etc.), and which ones will I make part of my life?

Who are the people who life me up and how will I surround myself with them? Who are the people who drain me, and how will I minimize my contact?

What messages will I read and share, and what practices will help me stay positive and spread hope?

Level 3: Mental energy:

What is most important right now and how will I prioritize that in my life? What will I let go of?

How will I help myself focus? What distractions will I stay away from, and what habits will I set in place?

How will I structure my workday to do blocks of deep work? How and when will I take breaks?

Level 4: Spiritual energy:

What are my top strengths, and how will I use them in my work and interactions with others?

What are my passions and interests and how I make time for them? How will I make time for play and laughter?

Which daily practices will help me stay connected to something larger (gratitude, mindfulness, etc.)? When will I do them?

Once you have a structure in place, do not, I implore you, try and turn over a new leaf overnight. It just doesn't work. The brain is an energy intensive machine and can only deal with a couple of small changes at a time. You'll fail miserably and either beat yourself up for something that's humanly impossible. Or you'll give up on yourself and go back to your old ways.

Always remember that easy does it. You lay the structure of your best life one brick at a time, just as you move toward your ideal self one step at a time.

STAYING PLUGGED IN

I began writing this book right before the 2020 pandemic. The initial days were a breeze—I had good structures in place and motivation was at its peak. Ideas sparked and my writing flowed. I hoped to be done in a few months—although that, I later found out, was amateur thinking.

Then the lockdowns happened, and life took a massive turnabout. My daily structure crumbled about my ears as all the four children came back home. We were five adults stuffed like sardines in my little downtown apartment, and we could literally hear each other breathe. With everyone needing a workspace, the only place I now had to do my writing was a little den with no sunlight. Some days, it was the bathroom, because it's mighty hard to think, when everyone is on work and school calls.

If that weren't enough of a challenge, my inner critic decided to join the party. She would sit right beside me at every writing session, pitying me, mocking me, or correcting my thoughts even before I'd quite written them down. I was crawling my way through the book and frustrated beyond measure.

That's when I remembered I could create an inner dream-maker just for my writing. I desperately needed her to get me through—and to do so with joy and vitality. And so I did. She was a mix of a muse from Greek mythology, and aunty Lathifa, my art teacher from childhood, and she brought a much-needed lightness to my work and life. Some days she would even ask me to wear my high heels and red lipstick when I sat down to work in my little den. "Why not?" she would say. "Let's pretend you're a famous writer!"

She also watched over my energy like a hawk. Every time it dipped, she'd come to the rescue: Am I sleeping enough, eating enough, laughing enough? Am I running around trying to be everything to everyone and forgetting that selflessness begins by acknowledging a self? Am I hooked into the idea of a *New York Times* bestseller and perfecting and tweaking the life out of my book? "It's called *Goodbye, Perfect* for a reason," she'd say with a wink.

Goodbye Perfect doesn't mean lowering your standards for work that is important. It means taking *yourself* less seriously, so you can take your work more seriously. It means—as rapper Jay-Z said—to treat your first as your last, and your last as your first. The inner dream-maker can help you do so, because she lives in a world of paradox, and is aware of your place in the larger flow of life: minuscule, yet essential.

I believe that having her by our sides is so important in a world that keeps demanding more from us at every turn, and where the feelings of control we once had have given way to chaos and uncertainty. Every little while, we need to remind ourselves of what's important, to take care of our minds and bodies, to nourish ourselves with what lifts us up, so we bring our joyous spirited selves to the world, and not our tired, burned-out selves.

Yes, we need our inner dream-makers when we lose motivation, so she can ask us what's missing and what our inner child doesn't like about the situation. We need her when we get frustrated and overwhelmed so she can check in to see what we're resisting and help us find an easier way to do things. And we need her when we just can't do it any more, so she reminds us that life is a continual falling back and stepping forth. It's how we engage with the *next* moment as our joyous, creative selves, as we bead the necklace of a purposeful life, one moment at a time.

SHINING TOGETHER

Early one morning, shortly after the beginning of the pandemic, I was lying in bed thinking about the state of the world. Life had just been thrown into chaos. The structures and systems we'd set in place were crumbling before our eyes. Women were hit the worst, and the advancements in gender parity made over centuries were headed in the opposite direction.

I was doing what I could to help. I had started free gatherings and sessions on Zoom where women could come together, talk about their challenges, feel understood, and less alone. I was offering workshops, tools, and talks I would normally charge for to help women work through their fears and anxieties. I'd doubled my writing and social media presence.

But it all seemed like a needle in a haystack. Women were suffering. And I kept feeling a sense of helplessness and hopelessness that wasn't helping, because I had my own challenges to deal with. My children were home from college and they too were struggling.

As I lay in bed, my thoughts racing through my head, I turned to the universe for guidance: "Please show me what I'm being called to do right now."

The sun was just about rising from behind the skyscrapers that surrounded our downtown apartment. My room was dark as night because my son, who was home from college because of lockdown, slept in the attached solarium and liked to shut the dividing door. I looked up, and I saw something on the ceiling that took my breath away. Far in one corner of the pitch-black ceiling, a tiny little heart shone brightly. *Love and light.*

Had the universe spoken? Was it telling me that I was a little speck in the world, one in billions? That the work of bettering the world was ours to do together, and I was trying to bite more than I could chew? Who knows why that bright little heart popped up on my ceiling and was gone before I could fully take it in. But it did bring me a sense of peace and a renewed commitment to my work, instead of the restlessness and scattered energy I was experiencing.

We are each a shining little heart engaged in the same collective purpose: to spread love and light through our unique gifts and capacities. It's how we engage with the world with big hearts and brave souls.

Chapter 7

Living with Courage

Now that you've built a sense of belonging, and have found your soul's purpose, you *are* going to be called to be courageous. You've stepped into the hero's journey, and your demons and dragons await you. Fear will be loud. Really loud. Unlike the emotion of awe we met in the previous chapter, this fear will cripple you because it's our oldest survival instinct. It will drag you into the abyss of despair. It will bring you down to your knees again and again. And you'll need a whole lot of courage to withstand it, so you come through to life a transformed and bigger version of yourself.

It's important to understand what courage means, because our world paints an image that's based on masculine traits and patriarchal values. Real courage, writes poet David Whyte is "not necessarily to go anywhere or do anything except to make conscious those things we already feel deeply and then to live through the unending vulnerabilities of those consequences."[79]

Psychologist Robert-Biswas Diener describes it as the willingness to act despite the fear.[80] It's showing up with a fluttering heart because you know the work is essential. It's having that important conversation despite the lump in your throat. It's voicing your idea in a meeting even though you fear you'll black out.

We tend not to think of these moments as courage because they don't often look and feel like it. When I look back on my life, my recovery from the eating disorder was courage. It was willing myself to eat multiple times a day despite ED freaking out or spewing hatred in my ears. It was watching the numbers increase on the scale and hearing people say I looked healthy without bursting into tears. Or bursting into tears and still having the next meal without cutting corners or skipping dessert.

We all have countless such moments in our lives. As women, we have even more of them because our lives are centered around relationships. And relationships feel vulnerable. There's nothing easy about opening your heart and sharing something personal when you have no idea how the other person will respond. Or listening to your child's hopes and dreams for their life when you know that life makes few promises, especially in a world in turmoil. The pandemic itself has been a collective test of courage; we've been lugging fear along as we go about our day, sometimes catching glimpses of it in our own fear-stricken faces on Zoom.

We forget these everyday moments of courage when we're called to step up onstage and take the spotlight. I forgot them the night I gave the fateful TEDx talk I wrote about in the introduction. Instead, fear grabbed the mic, turned the knob on full volume, and snuffed the passion out of my voice. My initial desire to change hearts and minds wasn't even a whisper in the background.

I share this story because almost all of us can think of times we were driven by a deep desire to make a meaningful difference but didn't come through as well as we could have because fear was grappling for the driver's seat. Or of times we did bolt through the back door because it had completely taken over. A few weeks ago, someone on my newsletter list sent me an email:

> I just turned down a really good job offer and have terrible regrets about it, but I had such anxiety and indecision, I just couldn't go forward. I'm trying to convince myself that it was for the best and meant to be, but I'm struggling to believe that good opportunities will come again. I keep doing this, and if nothing else, it's a sign that I really need to work on myself before I confront more decisions. It's so

hard sometimes to achieve what I want, or even know what I want, and I constantly live with an empty feeling. Life is so short and precious and I really want to make the most of it and do what I'm meant to do on this earth.

To do what we're meant to do on this earth, we need to have strategies to manage fear, because as Dr. Pippa Grange writes in her book *Fear Less:* "fearlessness isn't a strategy."[81] Without it, we can put ourselves in harm's way or fail to protect ourselves when we need to. It's why adolescence can be a time of impulsive actions, decisions that aren't thought through, and millions of needless accidents and premature deaths. For evolutionarily advantageous reasons, the brain in adolescence is biologically programmed to be somewhat disconnected from fear.

These days, with the endless fears and uncertainties we face, most people are caught in one of three camps. Some are so overwhelmed by the fear of what's to come that they find it difficult to function at their best on a daily basis. Others are carrying on like adolescents, blind to what's staring us in the face, because it's easier to pretend it doesn't exist.

And there are those who are engaged in purposeful action because they know how to buckle their fear safely in the back seat. They're strengthening their confidence because action, write authors Kathy Kay and Claire Shipman in their book

The Confidence Code, is the stuff of confidence.[82] Etymologically, confidence comes from the Latin verb *confidere* where *con* means "completely" and *fidere* means "to trust." When you keep your work to yourself and do what you set out to do, you build the confidence of I can do it! Even if you don't succeed, you build trust that you have what it takes to deal with whatever comes your way. In fact, research shows that failure is more correlated with mastery than success. **It's not the outcome that matters, it's the courage to act that does.**

As we begin courage-building work, it's important to note that courage grows through **three** essential steps:

> 1. The opportunity or idea takes hold. This is the primary focus of current confidence-building and leadership development work.
> 2. The moment of truth arrives. There's far less focus here, even though it's where women struggle the most.
> 3. The moment passes, well or not so well. There's almost no work in this space, and our best moments of courage do nothing for our confidence.

STAGE 1: THE CALL TO COURAGE

When you come up with an idea that sparks your energy, or an aspiration for yourself or for those around you, fear will try to nip it in the bud almost instantly. What's critical at this stage is to recognize the voice of fear, because fear is like a chameleon—it camouflages itself so you mistake it for the truth. It has been being doing this so damn well for millennia that the survival instinct is just as alive in our twenty-first-century brains as it was for our hunter–gatherer ancestors.

RECOGNIZING FEAR

These are some of the common hiding strategies fear uses to stop us from taking action. Or to do so *once we've made sure we will not fail or receive criticism*. That's the perfecting, pushing, controlling. The fixing, dotting the i's and crossing the t's so nothing falls through the cracks. We never get to test fear's hypotheses and stay addicted to the behaviors we long to let go of.

I've divided fear's hiding strategies into two categories—**impending disaster and the inability to deal with it**. Combine this survival instinct with voice of the firefighter (from chapter 4) and you have one hell of a dynamic duo.

"THIS WILL BE A DISASTER"

Everything and Always

It's when you latch onto something that went badly in your own life or someone else's or in the news and are convinced it's what's about to happen. A plane crashed or was hijacked, and now every flight you take becomes filled with dread. It's an all-or-nothing view of the world.

This cognitive distortion also tends to be accompanied by imagery of catastrophic outcomes or by a gut feeling that something's wrong. You may think it's intuition guiding you, your body telling you something important. But the reality is that it's almost impossible to listen to the voice of your deepest wisdom when fear has control of your mind and body.

The Comeback

We've all experienced this one—whatever you say to your fear, it comes back with yet another objection and you get thrown off again.

You: "I've prepared well and I've got the presentation under control."

Fear: "But not the Q&A, you can't prep for that".

You: "Nobody can, so it's a level playing field."

Fear: "That's what you think—people have so much more experience than you."

You: "That's not true, I was a start debater in college."

Fear: "College! You have to be joking. That's like thirty years ago?!"

You can never win with the Comeback.

Advice

Of all of fear's hiding strategies, this is undoubtedly the most cunning because we rationalize our inaction to ourselves. It often sounds like wisdom, reason, or practicality and tends to tap into your conscientiousness: "It's a great idea, but the kids need you right now." Or "Why don't you get another degree first because there's a lot of competition out there."

"YOU DON'T HAVE WHAT IT TAKES"

The Doubt

You doubt your competence, and much like "everything and always", you get hooked on all the moments where you failed to measure up to a task. The current task may not even be related to the previous ones, but fear will find a way to make the connection: "Are you sure you can do this negotiation thing with your manager. The last time you spoke to your teenager it didn't go that well."

The Scorn

This is perhaps fear's all-time favorite strategy in low or fragile confidence because it taps into the shame of unworthiness. It's the all too familiar "Who do you think you are?" often with a snicker or an incredulous shake of the head. And like "the comeback," you'll see all sorts of wild connections meant to make you feel small and insignificant: "You want that job? You can't even manage your weight."

The scorn can lead to physical withdrawal—you may suddenly slouch or feel your chin drop or shoulders droop. You may pull away from a partner or avoid eye contact–all bodily signs of shame.

Projected Pain

The thought of what you need to do will bring up memories from the past when you tried something similar and experienced the pain of rejection. Maybe you were criticized, maybe your efforts went unnoticed, or you walked away feeling unhappy with yourself. Remember, the inner manager's job is to protect you from past pain—it'll do everything to stop you in your tracks.

Sometimes the pain is so deep and persistent that you may experience a sense of drowsiness when you think about taking action. Or experience quite the opposite—restlessness and the need to do *some*thing in a frenzied state.

As you reflect on how fear speaks to you, you may want to think of whose voice or attitude it's adopting. It could be someone in your family, a caregiver, an older sibling perhaps. It could be the voice of your own limited awareness at the time, which helped you cope with a certain situation. Or it could the subtle and not-so-subtle messages you absorbed from the world around you, school, friends and teachers, or society. Knowing this helps you separate yourself from the voice of fear.

You'll likely also want to give it a name, because it helps you tune in to the voice of **the bigger you**. This was a key element of my recovery from the eating disorder, and I'd chosen to call it ED. During therapy sessions, when I'd share why I didn't do something I promised to do, my therapist would ask, "And whose decision was that?" If she sensed excuses and justifications, she'd say, "And who has the mic right now?" Or if I was hesitant to eat something that wasn't on ED's list, "What do *you* want?"

And yes, ED would get annoyed and whisper in my ear that my therapist was a little cuckoo. Its job, after all, was to keep me safe. It didn't give a flying fig about my dreams. Nor the fact that tomato risotto wasn't quite the same as a hungry tiger.

MANAGING FEAR

Once you've recognized and distanced yourself from the voice of fear, it's time to have a conversation with it, because remember, the job of the fear instinct is to keep you safe. Yes, it's overreactive, and yes, it's likely blind to your strengths and capabilities. But it may also be reminding you of important things we can forget when we're so drawn by our dreams.

We're not naturally adept at having this conversation because it was awfully disadvantageous to our ancestors. Imagine them thinking: "Hmm, I wonder if that's a real tiger in the bushes. You know what, let me wait and see. Who knows it may simply be a friendly deer. Actually, so what if it's a tiger? I'm sure I can shoo it away." You or I wouldn't be around today if they had put their thinking caps on.

These days though, we do need our thinking caps because our tigers are mostly *paper* tigers. Begin by asking your fear **"What are you trying to protect me from?"** and do not stop at the first answer. It is likely not the truth. Keep asking "and why does that matter?" or "is that a fact?" or "tell me more" until you arrive at something that feels a lot closer to the truth. Depending on the answer, here's what you can do:

Distance Yourself

If the fear is a figment of your imagination, you can safely turn a deaf ear by using its own weapon of choice: imagination. Here are a few of my favorite:

Turn down the volume: Pretend you're turning the volume dial down on the fear. Notice it becoming a little whimper in the background.

Walk fear out: Pretend you're holding it by the arm and walking it out the door. Or that you've bought it a ticket halfway around the world.

Throw it in the worry basket: Pretend you've got fear in your hand and are throwing it into a "worry basket" to return to at a later stage. Or you may want to write it out and tear it, burn it, bury it, or watch it float away.

If you think these strategies sound ineffective, think of how powerful the imagination is in creating horrific scenarios of doom and disaster. Why not use it to create something that's far better aligned with your goals?

Wear Your Parachute

If the fear is real, you'll need to do something to protect yourself. Think of it like putting on your parachute—you're still going for the dive, you're just making sure you don't land to your death. Here are some questions that can help:

Who will I reach out to?

What does plan B look like?

What have others done that I can learn from?

As you reflect on these, and other similar questions, focus on the absolute minimum safety gear. This is especially important for us perfectionists because we can spend years standing at the edge of the plane and still not feeling ready enough to dive.

Build Perspective

If the fear is exaggerated but persistent, you're going to calm it down by showing it the full story so it has room to transform. Here are ways to do so:

Think of times in the past when you did well at a similar task.

Think of the positive things others have said about your capabilities.

Think of the positive impact it'll have on the people you want to influence.

Think of the best that can happen and how you'll prepare for it.

Think of the most likely outcome and how you'll build on it.

Think of the worst that can possibly happen and how you'll cope with it.

Think of times in the past when you failed or when things went badly and how you moved on from it.

Test the Hypothesis

If the fear is based on projected pain from the past, you are going to test its hypothesis so you don't have to fight with it every time you want to do something. Say you want to take a break but fear tells you that you can't because you'll fall miserably behind or people will think you're lazy. These are rigid internal stories that are past their time. You let go of them is by doing exactly what fear doesn't want you to do. Take that break! Just don't snooze off for five hours at a stretch because you may just prove your fear to be right.

Things that you've never done are your areas of growth, because you don't know how to do them well *yet*. Whether it's taking breaks, setting boundaries or being less controlling, you have to identify the skills you need to develop, set structures that help you do so, and take one small step at a time.

STAGE 2: THE MOMENT OF TRUTH

The moment has arrived or is just around the corner. It's time for the conversation, to express your opinion at the team meeting or to present in front of your colleagues or board members. And boy, will fear be loud. Louder than it's ever been. For that hunter–gatherer brain of yours, you're standing face-to-face with the hungry tiger. And you don't need Einstein to tell you what to do.

In this moment of truth, fear will mostly rely on nonvocal strategies, because your cognitive capacities have shut down. Your entire physiology and psychology are geared to flee. Blood is flowing away from your brain and to your limbs. You can no longer convince yourself of why it's a good idea to proceed with your goal.

The night of the TEDx talk, I wasted much of my breath trying to argue with my fear. I reminded myself that I knew my script well, that it was easy to follow, and that I'd done many presentations. But it kept screaming like a distraught child:

"Make sure you don't cry! Look, look, you're about to cry!"

"Oh God, what if you trip and fall on the way to the stage!" The imagery was now stuck in my head.

By the time my name was announced, my legs felt like jelly, and a strange drowsiness loomed over me. And every moment thereafter was a battle with the voice in my head.

What I needed in those moments were noncognitive tools to manage the surge of hormones. This is so important for women, because relative to men, we tend to experience our emotions more strongly, and the negative ones more frequently. Studies show that men are just as likely as women to fear being found to be a fraud, but women's heightened emotions make it much harder to bring perspective around these thoughts.[83] This is even more true for those of us with anxious attachment.

Below you'll find four *non*cognitive tools to manage the swell of emotions so you don't become crippled by them.

Breathe Easy

The breath is the quickest and easiest way to bring yourself back to center when you feel anxious, afraid, overwhelmed, or stressed out. It sounds so basic that most of us don't do it. But here's the magic of the breath: it's the only part of your physiology that you can control. You cannot control your racing heart, the downstream flow to blood to your limbs, or the dumping of fight or flight hormones into your body—all of which are fueling the feeling that something is terribly wrong.

But when you slow your breath down and breathe from your belly (instead of fast and shallow so you can run at full speed), you inform your body that there's nothing to fear. Do so for a minute or two, because usually that's all it takes for an emotion to run its natural cycle, and soon enough, you'll start feeling centered. Your blood will return to your head, and you'll be able to hear yourself think.

Redirect the Fear

This is another great way to manage your emotions and is especially helpful in times when you need to do something bold and daring. You're simply redirecting the existing surge of hormones so you move from feeling frazzled and restless to feeling energized and empowered.

Have a mantra: Empowering mantras are a great way to pump yourself up. Find the one that works for you, and repeat it to yourself as often as needed. Here's one I love: "Bring it on!"

Invite courage in: This is similar to the invite love in practice in chapter 5. You're opening the door for a virtue that already exists in you—it simply needed your permission slip.

Improve your posture: You'll be surprised how little things like sitting up taller or holding your chin up or smiling with confidence can calm your fears almost instantly, because they use the body to influence our emotions.

Have an If/Then Plan

This one is great for behaviors we wish we didn't do, but in the moment, we do them anyway. Some people call them "kryptonites" because they're like the alien mineral that would deprive Superman of his powers.

Think of your own kryptonites—saying yes to your colleague when they put you out of your way when you really want to say no. Or changing the topic when your date says something intimate even though you would like to take the relationship further. It's only *after* the event that you wish you had responded differently.

One of the best ways around our kryptonites is to create an if-then plan. If-then plans were first developed by Peter Gollwitzer at New York University as a way to bypass an unwanted behavior by planning in advance what we'll do instead. "*If* I feel hungry when I come home from work, *then* I will choose a healthy snack from the top rack on my refrigerator." Or "*If* I feel scared when it's time to voice my idea at the meeting, *then* I will look at my colleague who always cheers me on."

If-then plans work because we use our conscious brains while we still have them—*before* the event—so we show up in ways that are aligned with what we really want.

Ride the Wave

This one has worked wonders in my life, and I offer it with the sincere hope that it'll help you finally say goodbye to the behaviors that you just haven't been able to let go of.

I first learned of it during my eating disorder recovery when the anorexia had morphed into bulimia, as often happens when a starved body decides to take matters into its own hands. The cravings came on like massive waves, and I'd devour every food I didn't otherwise allow myself until I was sick to my tummy. When I shared this with my therapist, she said, "Why don't you ride the wave like a surfer instead of becoming consumed by it?"

I later learned that it's a practice taken from the field of addiction treatment, because the surge of emotions is so strong that it's accompanied by impulsive behaviors. Many times, our need for perfection, to please, to control, to correct others *are* like addictions. We cannot tolerate not doing them, and knowing how to survive those intense moments without succumbing to the urge requires an understanding of how addiction works in the brain.

In her book *Dopamine Nation*, Dr. Anna Lembke explains that every time we engage in a behavior we find rewarding, there's a rise in the neurotransmitter dopamine in the brain.[84] Almost immediately, there's also an equal and opposite rise on the side of pain, because the brain is trying to maintain a relatively stable physiological equilibrium. This process is called *homeostasis*.

Behaviors become addictive when the amount of dopamine that's released is high, because the pain that follows is just as high. When we cannot manage the emotional surge of negativity, we do more of the high-inducing behavior, which leads to more pain, and the vicious cycle continues. Even if the reason we initially began the behavior is resolved, we'll continue unless we can break the high-low surge of emotions.

I had to learn not only how to ride the wave of a binge, but also to ride the wave of not chopping a slice of pizza into twenty pieces or choosing a small plate over a regular one. It didn't matter how much I was loved or how good I felt about my life. I still had to deal with the anguish in the moment.

If you're trying to let go of some of your fear-based behaviors, here are ways you can stay with the unease until your brain finds the stability it seeks. Because it eventually will. It always does.

Breathe through it.

Call a friend.

Doodle or draw.

Play with your pet.

Think of images that calm you.

Listen to music.

Go out in nature.

Dance.

Scream into a pillow.

Take a soothing bath.

Practice self-compassion.

Practice mindfulness.

Ask for help from a higher power.

Ask yourself what "big me" would do.

I particularly like this last one because it calls on the bigger version of you. **Because sometimes all that "little me" wants is for "big me" to take charge.**

STAGE 3: THE MISSED OPPORTUNITY

This is the work *after* the work—the one you likely never do. You gave the presentation despite trembling knees. You spoke up at the meeting even though it took all of you to do so. You had that tough conversation with your teenager, the one you'd been avoiding for weeks. What's going through your mind now?

If you're like most women, it's likely one or both of two things:

You're thinking about all the things that didn't go so well.

You're dismissing everything that did go well after all.

This *maximization* of failure (real or perceived) and *minimization* of success is fear's way of making sure you don't take the risk again. You survived once, even though it told you not to put yourself in harm's way. What are the chances you'll be lucky a second time around? And so you obsess over every little thing that was anything less than perfect and attribute everything that was actually good to luck or other people or a one-off event that's unlikely to ever happen again.

Thus the genesis of a lifetime of feeling like a fraud, also known as impostor syndrome. As we discussed in chapter 1, impostor syndrome is conscious awareness of incompetence, undeservedness, or not being "good enough" in the role you play or the task you do. The irony is that it's mostly seen in high-achieving individuals who have ample external evidence of their accomplishments, yet remain unconvinced that they deserve it. A 2020 KPMG study found that 75 percent of female executives across industries have experienced it in their careers.[85]

In her book *Own Your Greatness*, Dr. Lisa Orbé-Austin writes that continually undermining our achievements ("That trek up Machu Picchu? Oh, it was nothing!"), and focusing on the ways we didn't measure up ("I took far too many stops along the way") creates and feeds impostor syndrome.[86] Our successes are lost on us, and we stay trapped in a perpetual cycle of striving, perfectionism, and overwork that often leads to burnout. Or we shrink our comfort zones and live with the could've, should've, would've of our smaller lives.

To build the confidence we need to live our biggest lives, we have to take in what we did, regardless of how it turned out. We have to turn our attention to what went well, because we can't expect the brain's negativity bias to do so. And we have to put our failures into perspective, because self-perceptions happen to be mostly inaccurate in domains of self-worth dependency: what feels like success or courage in someone else will feel far less so in yourself.

When you take in your moments of competence, courage, or success, they sink into the deeper recesses of your implicit memory. As Dr. Rick Hanson writes in his book *Hardwiring Happiness*, passing states turn into lasting traits.[87] The better you get at savoring and celebrating your success, the more you close the gap between what you know about yourself and what you feel about yourself. You close the gap of fragile confidence.

Even so, this can be a challenge for women thanks to generations of gender socialization in our homes and societies. When I talk about the importance of celebrating ourselves and our achievements, there's always someone in the room who'll vocalize what's on everyone's mind: "But, Homaira, it doesn't feel right." They get it at a cerebral level, but their bodies seem to reject it. Invariably, they start talking about experiences they've had, of moments when the people they loved and looked up to failed to make them feel seen and special. Or told them to temper down their enthusiasm because it's important to "be modest."

I remember speaking about celebration at an agency that specializes in experience design. One of the attendees, a young artist, spoke about how her mother would react when she got ready to go out with friends back in high school. "I was sixteen, and I loved to dress up," she said with tears in her bright blue eyes. "But my mom was always like, why don't you wear that other dress? Or this one's too tight or too red. I haven't even told her I'm exhibiting in New York City, because she'll just change the topic or say something that will rub me the wrong way."

Within moments, others shared similar stories from their own lives. Mostly, they spoke about the slights of a culture that doesn't allow women to love themselves, celebrate themselves, or talk about their brilliance. There's an unspoken understanding that when we hate ourselves and our lives or play down our successes, we're somehow being "nice" or "good" by making others feel better about their own lot.

Nothing could be further from the truth. When we hide our successes and our moments of courage and goodness, they slip through our fingers as though they never happened. What sticks instead is the times we shied away from the call, turned down an opportunity, or showed up in a way that didn't do justice to our brilliance or our vision. And we never stop talking about those!

I wish we all grew up in homes where our caregivers wowed at our childish scribbles and cried: "That's the gorgeoustest painting I've ever seen!" I wish our mothers had set us an example of how to celebrate ourselves, and our sisters and friends had encouraged us to do so. We'd be far more comfortable talking about our lives and achievements, which in turn gives other women permission to do the same. Instead, we keep perpetuating the myth that we'll be disliked for it and wearing the badge of smallness with an air of self-righteousness. Who is it serving?

THE INNER CHEERLEADER

The inner cheerleader is the fourth and final inner presence, and her role is to help you celebrate wholeheartedly but also authentically. Because celebration isn't about "Ain't I great," although there is an element of that, given the fundamental psychological need to be "prized." *Did you see me?* the inner child wants to know. *Did you love what I did? Was it the best ever?* Prizing doesn't make a child big-headed or too full of themselves. Instead, it helps them own their worth so they don't go through life proving they're better than others or more entitled to praise and opportunities.

I love doing the inner cheerleader work with clients or in groups, because it always brings positive energy into the room. It's unbelievable how much we each long to be celebrated and how excited we get when we give ourselves permission to do so. Some of my clients want their inner cheerleader to be as colorful and zestful as the ones on the football field, pompoms and all. Others think of people they've known who made them feel seen, who spread positivity and inspired them to go for the best version of themselves.

As you create your inner cheerleader, imagine a presence who raises you up, not tears you down, because life does its share of tearing down. Imagine someone who high fives you when things go well, encourages you when you lose your motivation, and lifts you back up when you're down in the dumps. Imagine the voice that reminds you of your goals and shows you what you're capable of, because only then will you have the courage to go after your dreams.

S.I.N.G

Most of us need a step-by-step framework on *how* to celebrate, because the thought of becoming like the pompous male colleague down the corridor is enough for us to ditch the idea forever. The acronym is **SING**, hopefully easy to remember because it's about singing your praises.

See your efforts, achievements, or courage. Don't leave work or end your day thinking you got nothing done. Instead, make a list of everything you did, however insignificant or inconsequential you think it was. Include that email it took courage to write and the conversation you'd been avoiding for weeks. Also include the things that are still in progress, because seeing how far you've come helps you stop obsessing about how far you still need to go.

Internalize. Feel the warmth of pride, the lightness of joy, the sense of achievement that comes from having reached a milestone. You may want to be vocal about it too, as in:

"You go girl!"

"I'm so proud of you!"

"You totally got this!"

It's also important to think of similar moments from the past so you begin to see a pattern in yourself. It transforms *I did this* into *I am the type of person who does this*. You're updating your internal story.

Some of my high-achieving clients worry that feeling good about their performance will make them complacent or suppress their ambitions. This belief is perpetuated by competitive cultures that benefit from keeping employees constantly hungry for praise. What they miss is the simple feedback loop of celebration: it releases dopamine in the brain, which motivates us to repeat the behavior.

Notice what you did that led to your efforts or achievements. This builds off of Stanford professor Carol Dweck's work on the fixed vs. the growth mindset. Her research shows that when feedback is related to personal traits ("You're so smart/so intelligent/so kind"), it can cripple you because you're now burdened with the pressure to maintain it without knowing how to do so.[88] But when you identify the strengths you used, the actions you took, and the people you reached out to, you feel empowered to repeat the outcome. Here are questions that can help:

What helped you do what you did?

What was most joyful about it?

What would you love to do more of?

What were some of the qualities you showed?

What went particularly well for you?

What's most exciting about next steps?

What can grow through this?

Be **grateful** for the people and circumstances that helped with the outcome. I find gratitude to be the often overlooked yet essential component of cheerleading work for many reasons. First, it is the truth. You're undoubtedly standing atop many shoulders; hundreds of people have shaped the person you are today. It's easy to get caught up in those who hurt you or harmed you. Negativity is, after all, built into the human brain.

When you shift your focus to the people and circumstances that helped you, you experience the warmth of being supported by the universe. You feel a sense of belonging, and that feeds your confidence. You also feel compelled to give back in some small way, whether it's in giving credit where it's due, opening doors for others the way they were opened for you, or engaging in your work with renewed energy because an entire ecosystem is rooting for you.

An appreciation of a larger ecosystem also helps when we face disappointments, because placing ourselves at the center of our worlds is a double-edged sword. Yes, you claim all the credit for your success. But you also come down hard on yourself when things don't go well. Research shows that grateful people experience less of a low in failure, because they don't fall all the way from the skies.[89]

UNHOOKING FROM PRAISE

When we do the inner cheerleader work, I usually address a feeling that many of us are aware of in ourselves, or struggle with in others. It's being hooked onto praise. We (or they) just can't get enough of it.

I remember not too long ago, a client sharing an incident at work that had left her quite confused if not somewhat rattled. She and her boss had spent a few weeks preparing a new organizational chart that took into account the preferences and strengths their team of fourteen. A week prior to the official roll-out, they had a meeting with all of them where my client unveiled the changes that were to come. The team received them well and were generally excited. However, one of them raised a valid concern. The boss lost it.

Not only did she "lecture" the team on the time, energy, and effort it took to do such a "massive overhaul," she also shamed them, in particular the employee who had dared speak up, by expressing her disappointment at her lack of appreciation. My client, who was the manager, found herself caught in the middle, not sure whether to support her boss or take a stand for her humiliated team member.

The boss was a classic example of being hooked onto praise. It mostly happens for two very different reasons. Some people get so much praise growing up that they become dependent on it. I've often seen it in anxious attachment, where our perfection, pleasing, and approval-seeking makes people want to praise us all the time.

The other reason is quite the opposite: a lack of appreciation that is typical of avoidant attachment. Those who don't grow up being "prized" by their caregivers or made to feel special for their moments of joy and achievement end up with a hungry heart. They go about their lives expecting pompoms and high fives every step of the way. When they don't get them, they become demanding or manipulative. When they do get them, it never feels enough because it all goes right through the hole in their heart.

If you find yourself always on the hunt for a little more praise and a little more celebration, take it what's been given. Let it warm your heart. Let it sink in, so it can heal the hole that has been hurting for so long.

UNHOOKING FROM CRITICISM

Praise has a twin: criticism. When we're hooked onto praise, we're also highly vigilant of criticism. Some of us can be less obsessed by the praise we get (or don't get) but watch out for signs of criticism and often notice them even where they don't exist.

Unhooking from criticism is about learning to shift from "*I'm bad/wrong/stupid*" to "*my work needs improvement.*" It's about *de*personalizing the feedback. This is so important for many reasons.

One, negative feedback almost always has something of value to offer. It is also part of every worthwhile journey—there's no way around it. And unfortunately, women do receive more of it, and more *personally* critical feedback.

Here are some questions to help you *de*personalizing it:

Who is the person giving the feedback? Do they know me well enough to do so? Have they earned the right to do so?

What is my relationship with the person? Do I care about
the relationship? Do I need to take their feedback
into account?

What does the feedback tell me about their preferences?
What do they want to see more of/less of? How can I
do so that's also aligned with my values?

What will I do differently?

FACING DISAPPOINTMENT

There will be times in all our lives when we'll be hard pressed to find
anything to celebrate. In fact, if someone tries to point out the silver
lining or says, "I'm really proud of how hard you tried," we may be
just so close to offloading all our anger, frustration, or pain onto them.

Say you didn't get the job you worked so hard for, your boss
unfairly blamed you for the messy data that audit found suspicious,
or you didn't speak coherently at a meeting. Say your wedding got
postponed (again) because of, well, a pandemic, you feel you let a
parent down, or your child did something you never expected. Say
you looked at yourself in the mirror and didn't recognize the woman
you see, or you climbed on the bathroom scale and were shocked
to read the number. Or say it rained on the day you planned for
the picnic, or your friend didn't invite you to her birthday bash. Of
course, you're disappointed, even distraught. What next?

When life throws you darts, the work of the inner cheerleader isn't to sing your praises or twirl with the pompoms. Instead, it shows up much like the inner compassion, because its job is to stop you from throwing yourself the second darts of shame and blame. Because suffering, says a Buddhist proverb, lies in the second darts.

I found this out a long time ago, when I was expecting my twins. Everything was cruising along smoothly until I went for a regular checkup at twenty-two weeks. The contractions that I'd dismissed as cramps or bloating were for real; I had started to efface and was almost three centimeters dilated.

The doctors admitted me immediately. My husband was called in, and we were told to prepare for the ultimate nightmare: the arrival of two extremely premature babies who weighed 700 grams each. That's about the weight of a loaf of bread. The doctors detailed the prognosis of birth at twenty-two weeks, and the chances of survival and normal development.

We were looking at a 98.6 percent chance that one or both babies would be mentally or physically disadvantaged. *If* they were to survive.

Needless to say, I was in disarray. My entire world had been pulled from beneath my feet, and I was desperately trying to make sense of it all. The nurses hooked me up to every measuring device, and the beeps and screen displays worsened my mental state. I felt I'd been transported out of my body and was a helpless observer of my own life.

I saw doctors and nurses rush in and out. I saw everything moving really fast; there were sights and sounds but nothing was registering. Nor could I feel anything physically. I noticed I was in a hospital gown but didn't know how or when that happened. I felt numb. And in that state of numbness, I somehow made it through the night.

The next day, my husband asked a close friend, who was a stay-at-home mom at the time, to be with me until the end of his work day. He didn't want me to panic and felt her presence would be calming.

Well, it wasn't.

My heart started racing the moment I saw her enter the ward where I was one of four patients. She looked around in absolute panic, and as soon as she saw me, she darted toward me crying, "What happened?", followed by endless questions to which I had no answer. *Were you resting? Were you eating enough? Did you lift anything—I told you it's twins, you need to be extra careful. What do the doctors say? Are they worried?*

I think she saw the pain on my face because she toned down her inquiry. *It'll be okay, I'm praying for you. You just need to rest. I'll bring you home-cooked food, hospital food is terrible.* But her words weren't aligned with her facial expression or body language.

The contractions came back on and without thinking, I pressed the nurse call button beside my bed. The nurses rushed in with a tocodynamometer (the device that measures the length, frequency, and strength of uterine contractions), and my friend was asked to leave the room. Before leaving, though, she reassured me she'd come back every day to check in on me. I tried to resist, but she insisted, "What are friends for, silly?"

Even in that distraught state, I knew her presence—well-meaning as it was—was not what I needed. I called my husband immediately. "I need you to stop her from coming," I said. "I know she'll likely be upset, and it could damage our relationship. But this is the most important thing for our family right now."

I held the lesson I learned that day close to my heart throughout the twin's pregnancy. I drew very clear boundaries on who could visit and who couldn't in order to safeguard my mental state. And I went one step further. I also drew very clear boundaries on what I said or didn't say to myself. The incident with my friend had shown me what emotional reactivity or shaming and blaming can do. And my maternal instincts wouldn't allow it, even from myself.

The more I got on my own side, the more my body cooperated with me. Moment to moment, I tended to what it needed without thinking of the long journey ahead. Day by day, the twins developed key bodily abilities and neural perceptions such as sight and hearing. Slowly but surely—albeit with a few emergency visits to the labor ward—we moved closer toward a safe delivery and a healthy chance at life.

The doctors and nurses called me their miracle patient. They asked me what I was doing that defied medicine. I was mostly standing guard at the door of my mind.

The twins finally came into the world at thirty-four weeks, which is within the range of a normal twin pregnancy. They are now twenty-one; conscientious young adults who light up my life. Often when I watch them, or think of what could've been, I'm reminded of the importance of getting in touch with our consciousness protective parts, because they can quite literally help us experience heaven on earth.

～～～

We'll all face disappointments in life, and we'll need the clairvoyance and courage of our inherent wisdom to guide us. But we cannot access it when we're busy hammering down on ourselves or others. The research on post-traumatic growth shows that even in the midst of great psychological pain, some people are able to accept the stresses as a fundamental tenet of existence, stay mindfully with the experience, and thus engage their personal agency in making things better.[90] They are the people who don't play the shame and blame game.

So when life throws you the first darts, watch out for the second darts of your inner manager or inner firefighter:

"Why would they even want to hire me?"

"Everybody I know is in a relationship. Something must be wrong with me."

"I haven't hit one good shot so far, I'm a terrible player."

"I'll never get promoted because I have a family to look after. It just sucks."

"I'm unlucky with everything I try. I might as well stop trying."

Would you say any of this to a child who has just heard disappointing news? Wouldn't it completely break her if you did? Would you tell your toddler who keeps falling as she takes those wobbly first steps, "Everyone else is running already. What's wrong with you?" How motivated will she be to keep trying?

You are that toddler, that little child inside. Imagine the opportunities you'd seek if you weren't so hard on yourself for failing. Imagine the conversations you'd have if you weren't so afraid of disappointing someone or their disapproval and criticism. Imagine the love you'd express, the help you'd ask for, the dreams you'd pursue, if you weren't so quick in justifying why it's wrong or unwise to do so.

Confidence, says Paul Gilbert, is something we'd all have if we simply stopped criticizing ourselves so much. Because it's one thing to beat down on ourselves for hurting others or letting them down. As we saw in chapter 4, there may be evolutionary advantages to shame. But I cannot understand why we would come down so hard on ourselves for things done *to us*.

You may not be able to muster the energy to get back up when life knocks you down. But you can and must refuse to crush yourself with your own harsh words when you're already on the ground.

I promise that when you keep the noise down, you'll connect to your fiercest, boldest self. Because we all have her. When the stakes are high enough, we all have that intense matriarchal energy that lays down boundaries, that says "no more" to unfairness, that stands up for something bigger than ourselves. This is the soulful energy that's grounded in values of interdependence. And sometimes these values can clash among themselves.

Much as I valued and appreciated people's concern and desire to help during my pregnancy, I valued the health and happiness of our family *more*. In the years since, I've found that every time I've kept the mental clamor down, I've managed to connect to what's *more* important in the situation. There is immense wisdom inside each of us. We just can't hear it when the inner critic is banging on the doors and screaming in our heads.

CRAFTING YOUR LEGACY

Once you've gotten to know your inner cheerleader, make her a regular part of your life. Take her with you wherever you go, especially if you need encouragement to get through your day. And these days, who doesn't?

Time and again, friends and clients talk about lacking the will to brave a new day or longing for the hope and cheer they once had. They talk about dragging themselves through their days and not having the energy to initiate anything new or pursue long-cherished goals. I myself have lain in bed wondering where I'll find the motivation to get up and do the work I know I need to do.

Now more than ever, we need our inner cheerleaders to greet us in the morning and to accompany us through the day. We need her high fives, her reassuring smiles, her uplifting words, her comforting presence. We need her so we believe in ourselves and reengage with the work we each need to do in the world.

We also need her at the end of each day. Research shows that when our minds are quiet, we look for moments that make us proud.[91] When we shine the light on our wins instead of tormenting ourselves about all the things left undone or all the ways we fell short of some unattainable ideal, we create a story that does justice to who we are.

The reality is that none of us will hit a home run every day, or perhaps ever. But all of us do win at the little things many, many times a day. Getting the kids off to school on time. Speaking up in a meeting with a new team. Completing the project knowing it isn't perfect. Showing up with a smile even though the clothes don't fit. Getting out of bed after the tenth job rejection in a row. Making it through a trying day without completely losing it.

These are the marathons we run, the mountains we climb. These are the wins that accumulate over time and become the stories we reflect on at the end of our lives. With every small step, fist bump, and high five, you're writing your legacy. There's nothing trivial about that.

Part 4

Parting Words

Conclusion

As You Move On

I was an anxious person for most of my life. My English tutor in Sri Lanka used to call me a "worrier" and told me many times I'd make a good fiction writer. She wasn't applauding my writing skills. She was exhausted trying to tame my wild imagination that would create no end of *what if* scenarios.

One bottomless wellspring for my generative imagination was the regular family trips we would take from the coastal capital of Colombo, where we lived, to the hill stations. I loved the trips once we got there. The air was cool and crisp, the scenery was breathtaking, and the chefs in the rest houses would bake us scones for afternoon tea and serve them with homemade mulberry jam. What more could a little kid ask for?

The problem was *getting* to the hill stations. Almost four decades ago, the roads in the relatively underdeveloped country weren't exactly multilane highways. They were single lane, with barely any room between the outer wheels of a car and the sharp cliffs that dropped miles below. Many times, a descending car and an ascending one couldn't even pass each other—the ascending car had to reverse on the winding road until the road widened just enough to allow it. Even the thought of the treacherous journey often brought tears of panic to my eyes.

The only way I learned to survive the car ride was by keeping my eyes shut all the way. I didn't want to know when waterfalls gushed down rocky cliffs, when little children came selling bandannas and knick-knacks, or when monkeys were swinging and partying on plantain trees. What good were little joys when our lives were on the line?

As I've grown older, I've come to realize that it's these very joys that allow us to bear the fears and pains of human existence. Because no life is without them, and nobody promised us a smooth ride. And the ride is getting bumpier as we grapple with our current realities. Floods and fires are not just science and data but a landscape in flames, starving species falling from the skies, and social disparities that make it hard to look at ourselves in the mirror. We are facing the nightmare that was once the stuff of fiction.

To face it with the best of ourselves—because we're needed more than ever—we *have* to be present to the little joys that life offers us in plenty. The research on positive emotions shows that it's the little joys that help us manage anxiety because they build resilience. They help us stay engaged even when we feel cynical or hopeless and broaden our perspectives so that righteous anger doesn't turn into rage. Given the emotional heartbeat of our day and age, we obviously aren't paying attention to the countless ways the world around us nourishes the world within us.

Look around you. A stretch of blue sky. The way the light falls through the trellis. The silhouette of a tree at sunrise or the way it's twisted itself in search of light. Listen. The sound of birds chirping, the dryer doing its job, the construction down the road that reassures you life continues to hum along. *Feel* around you. The nip of morning freshness, the scent of the baby who just awoke from sleep or of the lavender bush that comes back year after year. Feel the sense of rightness within you in this moment or the delight of the toddler scampering after a butterfly and then searching for it in her tiny, clenched palms. There is so much to fuel us every moment of the day. Even man-made beauty is a source of joy when we learn to see with eyes that appreciate and a heart that is grateful.

We've become immune to these little joys in a world where entertainment is confused with enjoyment and where moderation is no longer a virtue. It takes courage to miss a party or not watch the "trending" show on Netflix. It takes courage to unsubscribe from twenty newsletters so you can actually read the one that speaks to you. FOMO—the fear of missing out—is a reality of our day and age. It went into hibernation during the pandemic, when sitting at home was what everyone was doing. But once things started opening up again and social life began creeping back in, friends and clients shared the anxiety of having to be everywhere all the time. FOMO was a thing again.

Fear also creeps in because opening our hearts to the little joys shines light on the questions we bury at the bottom of our awareness as we carry on in life. What does it mean to be a good human? What does it mean to live a good life? It takes courage to address these questions, because courage, writes David Whyte, is "the measure of our heartfelt participation with life, with another, with a community, a work; a future."[92] It's easier to go back to pursuits that are at best a backdrop to life. **They're never the point of it**.

The good news is that we're ready to address the point of it. Our conversations with ourselves and with each other are increasingly about the emptiness of living on the surface. Even millennials are tiring of the notion of progress as proud independence and not just questioning but rejecting the need for more accumulation, more success, more rationality. In her latest book *Beautiful*

World, Where Are You?, author Sally Rooney writes of the millennial angst and of an emerging appreciation of interdependence as the very purpose of life.[93] More and more, we're attracted to community, to relationships, and to the call to engage with the present moment as a way to live fully *despite* a crumbling world.

Throughout our collective evolution, we've arrived at thresholds that have demanded more of us, biologically or culturally. I believe that right now, we stand at a threshold again. The ecological disasters, the social strife and inequality, the steady loss of an ecosystem that supported life on earth are visible manifestations of an internal loss, that of our core.

For too long, we've been living in a loveless stupor, caught between our endless urgencies and hopeless withdrawal. For too long, we've bought in to the fervor of stimulating entertainment and frantic improvement and forgotten that life begs our presence to its wonders. For too long, we've believed the story of unchecked independence and undone the fabric of human dependency that cradled us at every stage of our collective growth.

And we've lost our souls, even as we've adulated the self.

The call right now is to reconnect with who we truly are. To return to a more joyous, more compassionate, more collaborative engagement with ourselves and the world. To stop scraping the remains of our beleaguered planet and to start attuning with life's abundance and to the people—past, present, and future—who are central to our narrative.

As women, we are the natural team of change makers. Whether we like it or not, we've been selected to advance our humanity to the next stage of our common journey. We're being called to assist our planet through its transition into adulthood, because that's where we find ourselves. We have, I believe, reached a collective middlescence, the second major transition in life that integrates the energy of adolescence with the wisdom of experience.

Middlescence is not a biological age—we can live our entire lives focused inward or attached to theoretical ideals. As Maya Angelou writes, "Most people don't grow up. It's too damn difficult. What happens is most people get older. That's the truth of it. They honor their credit cards, they find parking spaces, they marry, they have the nerve to have children, but they don't grow up. Not really. They get older. But to grow up costs the earth, the earth. It means you take responsibility for the time you take up, for the space you occupy. It's serious business. And you find out what it costs us to love and to lose, to dare and to fail. And maybe even more, to succeed."[94]

At its core, middlescence is about appreciating life's paradox so we can give ourselves fully to it. Because all life *is* a paradox.

It always has been. There's beauty despite the burning, joy amid fear and grief, agency even when things are outside our control. There are few facts and many opinions, and growing up is about holding on to multiple opinions at the same time.

Dr. Robert Kegan, who created the constructive developmental framework that describes the five stages of growth into adulthood, calls this the fifth stage of adult development. His research shows that up to 70 percent of the educated adult U.S. population is stuck in the earlier stages—in the dogged pursuit of autonomy and the need to have arrived or an inability to take a stand for what we want without worrying so much about what others would think.

This collective stuck-ness is a reflection of our individual stuck-ness. "To grow into adulthood as a social species, including humans," writes John Cacioppo, who researches loneliness and belonging, "is not to become autonomous and solitary, it's to become the one on whom others can depend."[95] It's the unspoken premise of democracy; our independence is only as important as our concern for the common good. Without it, it's called *selfishness*.

The more we can embrace the paradox of life, the better we'll be able to brave its ups and downs until we learn do so with some grace. It's the only way to cope in a perfection-crazed world that deals with the negative, weaknesses, ambiguity, uncertainty, and chaos by denying them or fixing them. Neither is an option going forward, and dark clouds of hopelessness are converging upon us.

Paradox, on the other hand, is the birthplace of hope. And we need hope now more than ever. We need hope so we can keep planting the seeds even if they don't bloom in our lifetime. We need hope so we can stay tender with others even if their hearts need time to soften. We need hope so we can stay present to the everyday joys and not only live fully but also *give fully* to the world.

The people who do grow up are those who take responsibility for the fact that there's a life to be lived alongside the certainty of death that no one can evade. A life that longs for the human experience and wants to feel its everyday troubles and delights. It wants to have lived, to have felt, to have loved, not just ourselves but also the world. Because as Joanna Macy, author and environmental activist, writes in her book *World as Lover, World as Self*, the world is ourselves.[96]

A wholehearted life is not for the weakhearted, the mask wearers, and the gold-star collectors. It's not for those of us who go through life with our eyes shut and sensibilities numbed, waiting for the hill station. It's not for the worriers who spend more time in an imaginary world that ill equips us for the magic of the real one.

It took me much of my life to drop the label of *worrier* and to replace it with that of *warrior*. That is *the* label I want for you, dear reader. We're all warriors of the human spirit, driven by the desire to live fully and leave a lasting impact in some small and meaningful way. And more and more, we're realizing that to do so, we have to lean in to the moments that bring us joy and make them an integral part of our lives.

I want to leave you with a simple structure to do so, so when you close the book, you walk away with a plan to live—truly live—your precious and magical life.

LIVING YOUR IDEAL LIFE

A key lesson I learned from my confidence work is that we've been pursuing our best lives in the inverse direction. We think of what we ideally want of our lives, and then we work backward to what we need to change in order to live them.

Inherently, there's nothing wrong with that. Our ideals are usually an extension of our truth. But of course, that truth can be elusive in a noisy and demanding world. What we thought was *our* ideal life can leave us feeling empty and unfulfilled.

A better way is the matriarchal way: to begin with our sources of joy and inspiration and structure our lives in alignment with them. This is the essence of appreciative inquiry—a methodology of change that dreams of *what could be* based on the discovery of *what gives life*.

The four-step framework below will not only bring you joy and meaning, it will also build your confidence. Because confidence comes from knowing you're doing the things that are aligned with the person you truly want to be.

Step 1: Think of everything that helps you feel present, alive, and engaged with life. What are you thinking? What are you doing? How are you relating with others? What passions, qualities, and values do these point to? There is no right or wrong answer, so give yourself permission to be honest with yourself.

Step 2: Dream of your ideal day when these feelings, thoughts, and behaviors are an integral part of your life. What's different about it? How do you start and end your day? How much time do you spend on the things that are important to you? Who are the people you surround yourself with? How do you walk, talk, move, engage?

Step 3: Think of what you will need to change to make your dream a reality. As you think about the changes, also reflect on what you'll need to keep (because there's a lot that's right about your life) and what you'll make peace with (because *every*thing isn't in your control). What will you start doing and/or thinking (or do more of)? What will you stop doing and/or thinking (or do less of)? What will you maintain? What will you accept?

Step 4: Think about how you will set yourself up for success. What will you do to make sure the changes are easy to remember and incorporate in your life? What are the habits you'll set up? What are the challenges that can come up? How will you work through them? Are there mantras, quotes, or jujus that can act as reminders? Who can support you? How will you hold yourself accountable?

Having a framework will help you live with intention instead of blowing with society's gusts and breezes and chasing dreams that never belonged to you in the first place. This is your slender repertoire of agency. Because it *is* slender. We're born without choosing to do so. We don't choose our bodies, our brains, or our tendencies. We don't choose our parents, our history, or the circumstances we're born into. We don't choose life's twists and bends, nor the day it all ends. But we do get to choose how we embrace it all with gratitude and give it all we've got.

That is your greatest gift to life, for the gift of life. Remember, the universe chose you to be the one in millions who chanced to be born in that moment of conception. Remember, it loves you enough to nourish you every day with air, bread, loving relationships, and a unique gift that the world is hungry for. Will you now love yourself enough to receive it all with open arms and spread your love and light in the world?

Ultimately, that's confidence. There's no greater gift you can give yourself.

Acknowledgments

Goodbye, Perfect has been a journey, both as a framework and the mental time travel into my personal life, the people I've grown up with, and those whose work and research has guided and informed my own.

To the circle of life:

Needless to say, my work stands on the shoulders of giants—people whose lives have inspired me, whose ideas have influenced me, and whose presence makes our world a better place. In particular, a huge bow of gratitude to the late Michael Kernis whose research on fragile and optimal self-esteem changed my understanding of confidence forever. If not for your contribution to the scientific literature, I would've never understood why confidence can sometimes look like such an undesirable quality, nor why it is so essential to our lives and legacy.

Thank you too to all the researchers, practitioners, and those who help us live the soulful and heart-centered lives we want to live. Rick Hanson, Brené Brown, Rich Roll, Parker Palmer, Tara Mohr, Arianna Huffington, Maria Shriver, Tara Brach, David Whyte, Mark Nepo, Gail Brenner—I could go on endlessly. Some of you I know personally, and some of you are the words and voices that have been my lifelines in times of confusion and despair.

This section also needs a moment of grateful silence for all the people who were part of my younger days and who have now passed on. Thank you for your words, advice, and laughter that haven't faded over the years. I'm so blessed to have received your love.

My dearest Dadima, your love lives in every cell of my body and always will. I'll forever be grateful for your presence in my life that grounded me, that provided a safe refuge for my fearful mind, and that made me feel special in the most life-giving way. To this day, I can feel the warmth of those memories.

To the women in my life:

I have to begin with the wonderful women I've had the privilege to work with, especially in the Goodbye Perfect Program. You inspire me every day with your big hearts and soulful dreams and make me even more committed to helping you bring them to life. Thank you for your stories, many of which are in the book, and your insights that have expanded my own perspective and taught me the wisdom and beauty that's inherent in women's circles. Keep believing in yourselves and going after your dreams!

To the dear friends with whom I've shared laughter and tears and everything in between over the years. You know who you are. Thank you for always lending your shoulders, smiles, and sanity. A very special thank you to Sandra, my soul-sister who found me in the most magical way. I love you, I honor you, and I deeply treasure our friendship.

To the book birthing team:

To my incredible agent Linda Konner, without whom none of this would have been possible. You took a chance on a naive first-time author and believed in my story. Thank you for the endless rounds of edits even before you signed me on. You are the greatest dream-maker I could've asked for!

Thank you to the entire team at Sourcebooks for guiding me through every step of the book publishing process: Sarah Otterness, Sabrina Baskey, Kelly Lawler, Jillian Rahn, thank you for raising the book every time you touched it. And most of all, Meg Gibbons, my dear editor, whose clarity, insights, and patience with a writer who couldn't stop embellishing her work deserve the most heartfelt of thank-yous. I'm truly grateful to you for refining my thinking while holding space for my authentic expression.

To the people I can never thank enough:

To my parents first of all, not a day goes by when my heart

doesn't overflow with gratitude for your presence in my life. You show me how to love without fear, and how to do this impossible thing called parenting with grace. Thank you for your endless prayers, for your advice whenever I've asked for it, and for refraining from advice when I haven't. Thank you for being my cheerleaders as I connect more deeply with my authentic self and for believing in my ideas even before they fully take shape. As a parent myself, I know the courage it takes.

To my husband, thank you for the lesson you taught me in the very early days of our marriage: "You are a 99 percent wife and that is good enough." Who knew *Goodbye, Perfect* was born on that day—it took me all these years to stop trying to be 100 percent!!

To my brothers for their check-ins and encouragement, and to my little niece who wrote many books alongside me because she wants to be an author "just like phuppo."

And to my children—the loves of my life. I don't know how many times I've written this section and erased it again and again because words cannot express what you mean to me. If I haven't told you enough how proud I am of you, of your humanity, your brilliance, your humor, and your hearts of gold, it's because words fail my heart. You are my heart, my four chambers. May you always shine your love and light in the world.

Notes

1   Micheal Kernis, "Toward a Conceptualization of Optimal Self-Esteem," *Psychological Inquiry* 14 (2003): 1–26.

2   Susan Cain, *Bittersweet: How Sorrow and Longing Make Us Whole* (New York: Crown, 2022)

3   Lisa Miller, *The Awakened Brain: The New Science of Spirituality and Our Quest for an Inspired Life* (New York: Random House, 2021)

4   Ken Wilber, *Integral Meditation: Mindfulness as a Path to Wake Up, Grow Up, and Show Up in Your Life* (Boulder, Shambhala Publications, Inc., 2016).

5   Nick Schubert and Anne Bowker, "Examining the Imposter Phenomenon in Relation to Self-Esteem Level and Self-Esteem Instability," *Current Psychology* 38 (2019): 749–755.

6   David Hume, "Of the Influencing Motives of the Will," (Book III, Part III, Section III) in *A Treatise on Human Nature* (London, Longmans Green, and Co., 1878).

7   Rick Hanson, *Hardwiring Happiness: The New Brain Science of Contentment, Calm and Confidence* (New York: Harmony Books, 2013)

8   Diana Bilimoria and Deborah O'Neil, "Women's Career Development Phases: Idealism, Endurance, and Reinvention," *Career Development International* 10 (2005).

9   Rebecca Solnit, "Men Who Explain Things," *Los Angeles Times*, April 13, 2008, https://www.latimes.com/archives/la-xpm-2008-apr-13-op-solnit13-story.html.

10 Corinne Moss-Racusin, John Dovidio, Victoria Brescoll and Jo Handelsman, "Science Faculty's Subtle Gender Biases Favor Male Students," *Psychological and Cognitive Sciences* 109 (2012): 16474–79.

11 Carrie Arnold, *Silenced and Sidelined: How Women Leaders Find Their Voices and Break Barriers* (Maryland: Rowman & Littlefield, 2020)

12 Jonathan Haidt, *The Happiness Hypothesis: Finding Modern Truth in Ancient Wisdom* (New York: Basic Books, 2006).

13 Corinne Purtill, "If Winter Feels Extra Hard This Year, You're Not Alone," *The New York Times,* April 18, 2021, https://www.nytimes.com/2021/02/18/us/winter-stress-sadness-exhaustion.html.

14 Anthony de Mello, *Awareness: The Perils and Opportunities of Reality* (New York: Crown Publishing Group, 1990).

15 Mary Ainsworth and Silvia Bell, "Attachment, Exploration, and Separation: Illustrated by the Behavior of One-Year-Olds in a Strange Situation," *Child Development* 41 (1970): 49–67.

16 Walt Whitman, "Song of Myself," (51) in *Leaves of Grass* (London, 1886).

17 "2022 State of the Gender Pay Gap Report," *Payscale*, https://www.payscale.com/research-and-insights/gender-pay-gap/.

18 Stanford Encyclopedia of Philosophy, "Plato's Ethics: An Overview" revised December 06, 2017, https://plato.stanford.edu/entries/plato-ethics/.

19 Fabiana Fondevila, *Where Wonder Lives: Practices for Cultivating the Sacred in Your Daily Life* (Rochester: Findhorn Press, 2021).

20 Robert Augustus Masters, *Spiritual Bypassing: When Spirituality Disconnects Us from What Really Matters* (California: North Atlantic Books, 2010).

21 *Maria Shriver's Sunday Paper*, "Let's Get Angry," June 6, 2021.

22 Jeremy Lent, *The Web of Meaning: Integrating Science and Traditional Wisdom to Find Our Place in the Universe* (Canada, New Society Publishers, 2021).

23 "Leaders in Crisis: Attending to the Shadow Side," February 2016, http://www.erikdehaan.com/wp-content/uploads/2016/02/9780749468316_Chapter-8-unsecured.pdf.

24 Fenton Johnson, "Eudora Welty: All Serious Daring Starts from Within," *The Georgia Review 66* (Spring 2012): 52–61.

25 Margaret Wheatley, *Who Do we Choose to Be? Facing Reality, Claiming Leadership, Restoring Sanity* (Oakland: Berrett-Koehler Publishers, 2017).

26 Francoise Verges, *A Decolonial Feminism* (London: Pluto Press, 2021).

27 Jonathan Brown and Margaret Marshall, "The Three Faces of Self-Esteem," in M. Kernis (Ed.), *Self-Esteem: Issues and Answers* (New York: Psychology Press, 4–9).

28 Jonathan Brown, Keith Dutton, and Kathleen Cook, "From the Top-Down: Self-Esteem and Self-Evaluation," *Cognition and Emotion* 15 (2001): 615–631.

29 James Clear, *Atomic Habits: An Easy and Proven Way to Build Good Habits and Break Bad Ones* (New York: Avery, 2018).

30 Linda Hartling, Wendy Rosen, Maureen Walker, and Judith Jordon, "Shame and Humiliation: From Isolation to Relational Transformation," Stone Centrer Working Paper Series, 2000.

31 Paul Rozin, Jonathan Haidt, and Clark McCauley, "Disgust: The Body and Soul Emotion," in T. Dalgliesh and M. Power's (Eds.) *Handbook of Cognition and Emotion* (John Wiley & Sons, 1999).

32 Brené Brown, *Dare to Lead* (New York: Random House, 2018), 89.

33 Marc Brackett, *Permission to Feel: The Power of Emotional Intelligence to Achieve Wellbeing and Success* (New York: Celadon Books, 2019).

34 Alex Pattakos and Elaine Dundon's *Prisoners of Our Thoughts: Viktor Frankl's Principles for Discovering Meaning in Life and Work* (Oakland, Berrett-Koehler Publishers, 2017).

35 Maya Angelou, "A Brave and Startling Truth," composed for the 50th anniversary of the United Nations in 1995.

36 Jonathan Haidt, *The Happiness Hypothesis: Finding Modern Truth in Ancient Wisdom* (New York: Basic Books, 2006).

37 Colleen Hoover, *It Ends with Us* (New York: Atria, 2016).

38 Paul Gilbert and Sue Proctor, "Compassionate Mind Training for People with High Shame and Self-Criticism: Overview and Pilot Study of a Group Therapy Approach," *Clinical Psychology and Psychotherapy* 13 (2006) 353–379.

39 Mary Oliver, "To Begin With, the Sweet Grass," *Evidence: Poems* (Boston: Beacon Press, 2010).

40 Stephen Porges, "The Polyvagal Theory: New Insights into Adaptive Reactions of the Autonomic Nervous System," *Cleveland Clinical Journal of Medicine* 76 (2011): 86–90.

41 Shauna Shapiro, *Good Morning, I Love You: Mindfulness and Self-Compassion Practices to Rewire Your Brain for Calm, Clarity, and Joy* (Boulder: Sounds True, 2020).

42 Tamara Ferguson, Heidi Eyre, Michael Ashbaker, "Unwanted Identities: A Key Variable in Shame–Anger Links and Gender Differences in Shame," *Sex Roles* 42 (2000): 133–57.

43 Kristen Neff, *Fierce Self-Compassion: How Women Can Harness*

Kindness to Speak Up, Claim Their Power, and Thrive (New York: Harper Collins, 2021).

44 Daniel Ladinsky and Ḥāfiẓ, *The Gift: Poems by Hafiz* (New York: Penguin Books, 1999).

45 J. Prims and D. Moore, "Overconfidence over the Lifespan," *Judgment and Decision Making* 12 (2017), 29–41.

46 John Powell, "The Mechanisms of Othering," YouTube, 2015, retrieved December 13, 2022, from https://www.youtube.com/watch?v=Cs3mtCqC8S4.

47 M. Buber and J. Yang, *Ich und Du* (Gütersloh: Gütersloher Verlagshaus, 1999).

48 The Omega Institute for Holistic Studies, "Pema Chödrön: This Lousy World," YouTube, September 13, 2008, retrieved December 13, 2022, from https://www.youtube.com/watch?v=buTrsK_ZkvA.

49 Richard Shell, "Bargaining Styles and Negotiation: The Thomas-Kilmann Conflict Mode Instrument in Negotiation Training," *Negotiation Journal* 17(2001) 155–174.

50 Jennifer Crocker and Amy Canevello, "Creating and Undermining Social Support in Communal Relationships: The Role of Compassionate and Self-image Goals," *Journal of Personality and Social Psychology* 95 (2008), 555–575.

51 Daniel Pink, *To Sell is Human: The Surprising Truth about Moving Others* (New York: Riverhead Books, 2012).

52 Tara Mohr, *Playing Big: Practical Wisdom for Women Who Want to Speak Up, Create, and Lead* (New York: Avery, 2015).

53 James Pennebaker, "Writing to Heal: A Guided Journal for Recovering from Trauma and Emotional Upheaval," *Center for Journal Therapy*, 2004.

54 Helen Keller, *The Story of My Life* (New York: Dover Publications, 1996).

55 Meg Warren, Tejvir Sekhon, and Rachael Waldrop, "Highlighting Strengths in Response to Discrimination: Developing and Testing an Allyship Positive Psychology Intervention," *International Journal of Wellbeing* 12 (2022): 21–41.

56 Shelley Gable, Gian Gonzaga, and Amy Strachman, "Will You Be There for Me When Things Go Right? Supportive Responses to Positive Event Disclosures," *Journal of Personality and Social Psychology* 91 (2006): 904–917.

57 Daniel Kahneman, Olivier Sibony, and Cass Sunstein, *Noise: A Flaw in Human Judgement* (New York: Hachette, 2021).

58 Daniel Pink, *The Power of Regret: How Looking Backward Moves Us Forward* (New York: Riverhead Books, 2022).

59 Quoted in Robert Furey, *The Joy of Kindness* (Pennsylvania: Crossroad Publishing, 1993).

60 Jonathan Gustin, "The Triple Purpose of Life," YouTube, 2017, retrieved December 13, 2022, from https://www.youtube.com/watch?v=OaF5bvHoPkw.

61 Richard Rohr, *Falling Upward: A Spirituality for the Two Halves of Life* (San Francisco: Jossey-Bass, 2011).

62 Abraham Maslow, *Motivation and Personality* (Boston, Addison-Wesley Educational Publishers, 1998).

63 Parker Palmer, *A Hidden Wholeness: The Journey Toward an Undivided Life* (San Francisco, Jossey-Bass, 2004).

64 Stephen Batchelor, *The Art of Solitude* (New Haven, Yale University Press, 2020).

65 Rosa Parks, *My Story* (New York: Puffin Books, 1992).

66 Mihaly Csikszentmihalyi, *Optimal Experience: Psychological Studies of Flow in Consciousness* (New York: Cambridge University Press, 1988).

67 Gordon, Stellar, Anderson, McNeil, Loew, and Keltner, "The Dark Side of the Sublime: Distinguishing a Threat-based Variant of Awe," *Journal of Personality and Social Psychology* 113 (2017): 310–328.

68 Marianne Williamson, *A Return to Love: And the Gift of Change* (San Francisco: HarperOne, 2004).

69 Daniel Ladinsky and Ḥāfiẓ, *The Gift: Poems by Hafiz* (New York: Penguin Books, 1999).

70 Paulo Coelho and Alan Clark, *The Alchemist* (San Francisco: HarperOne, 1993).

71 Mary Oliver, *Blue Pastures* (New York: Harcourt, 1995).

72 Mirabai Starr, *Wild Mercy: Living the Fierce and Tender Wisdom of the Women Mystics* (Louisville: Sounds True, 2017).

73 T. L. Heath, *The Works of Archimedes* (New York: Dover Publications, 2002).

74 Greg McKeown, *Effortless: Make It Easier to Do What Matters Most* (New York: Penguin, 2021).

75 Bill Moyers, *Joseph Campbell and the Power of Myth*, interview with Joseph Campbell, 1988, retrieved from https://www.imdb.com/title/tt0296362/.

76 Kahlil Gibran, *The Prophet* (New York: Alfred Knopf, 2008).

77 Jim Loehr, and Tony Schwartz, *The Power of Full Engagement: Managing Energy, Not Time, Is the Key to High Performance and Personal Renewal* (New York: The Free Press, 2005).

78 Annie Dillard, *The Writing Life* (New York: Harper Perennial, 2013).

79 David Whyte, *Consolations: The Solace, Nourishment and Underlying Meaning of Everyday Words* (Washington: Many Rivers Press, 2015).

80 Robert Biswas-Diener, *The Courage Quotient: How Science Can Make You Braver* (San Francisco: Jossey-Bass, 2012).

81 Pippa Grange, *Fear Less: How to Win at Life without Losing Yourself* (London: Vermilion, 2021).

82 Kathy Kay and Claire Shipman, *The Confidence Code: The*

Science and Art of Self-Assurance–What Women Should Know (New York: HarperBusiness, 2018).

83 Nolen-Hoeksema and Jackson, "Mediators of the Gender Difference in Rumination," *Psychology of Women Quarterly* 25 (2001): 37–47.

84 Anna Lembke, *Dopamine Nation: Finding Balance in the Age of Indulgence* (New York: Dutton, 2021).

85 "Advancing the Future of Women in Business," KPMG, Women's Leadership Summit, 2020.

86 Lisa Orbé-Austin and Richard Orbé-Austin, *Own Your Greatness: Overcome Impostor Syndrome, Beat Self-Doubt, and Succeed in Life* (Berkeley: Ulysses Press, 2020).

87 Rick Hanson, *Hardwiring Happiness: The New Brain Science of Contentment, Calm and Confidence* (New York: Harmony Books, 2013).

88 Carol Dweck, "The Journey to Children's Mindsets-and Beyond," *Child Development Perspectives* 11:139–144.

89 Summer Allen, "The Science of Gratitude," May 2018, a white paper prepared for the John Templeton Foundation by the Greater Good Science Center at UC Berkeley.

90 Landi, Pakenham, Matioli, Crosetti, Agostini, Grandi, and Tossani, "Post-Traumatic Growth in People Experiencing High Post-Traumatic Stress during the Covid-19 Pandemic: The Protective Role of Psychological Flexibility," *Journal of Contextual Behavioral Sciences* 26 (2022): 44–55.

91 Alvin Powell, "Harvard Researchers Study How Mindfulness May Change the Brain in Depressed Patients," *Harvard Gazette*, April 9, 2018, https://news.harvard.edu/gazette/story/2018/04/harvard-researchers-study-how-mindfulness-may-change-the-brain-in-depressed-patients/.

92 David Whyte, *Consolations: The Solace, Nourishment and Underlying Meaning of Everyday Words* (Washington: Many Rivers Press, 2015).

93 Sally Rooney, *Beautiful World, Where Are You* (New York: Picador, 2021).

94 Maya Angelou, in an interview for *The Paris Review* no. 116, Fall 1990, retrieved from https://liberalarts.org.uk/most-people-dont-grow-up-maya-angelou/.

95 John Cacioppo, "The Lethality of Loneliness," TEDxDesMoines transcript, published electronically September 9, 2013.

96 Joanna Macy, *World as Lover, World as Self: Courage for Global Justice and Ecological Renewal* (Berkeley, Parallax Press, 2007).

About the Author

Homaira Kabir is the founder of the Goodbye Perfect Project, a bottom-up journey to women's leadership based on her postgraduate psychological research on confidence. Her passion for elevating women's voices and presence is complemented by her understanding of what confidence is (and isn't). Through her early experience with an eating disorder that she shares in the book, Homaira explains why the inner work of optimal confidence is essential for letting go of perfection, pleasing, and proving. She holds a double master's degree in positive psychology and coaching psychology from the University of East London. Her writing has appeared in *Forbes, Happify, The Huffington Post*, and *Thrive*, among others. She is married with four beautiful children who are the love and inspiration of her life.